The House of Hope

I had the privilege of going to China and witnessing the work that God is doing through Robin and Joyce Hill. They are wonderful servants of God who lovingly care for the "least of these". I hope that many will read this book and consider their example.

— **Francis Chan,** author of *Crazy Love*

This is a wonderful book. It tells how God works through us to save the weakest of the weak, bringing people together from across the world to build families in amazing and miraculous ways. It can only encourage all who love to read about God's grace, His faithfulness and His love for all people.

— **John Mumford,** National Director, Vineyard Churches UK and Ireland

Virgin Atlantic is extremely privileged to be associated with the Hope Healing Home and the inspirational, humbling work of Joyce and Robin Hill and their amazing team. All of us are proud of our relationship with the New Hope Foundation and are in awe of the dignity, kindness and love which those special people who work at the Home share with the special children in their care.

— **Jonathan Harding,** General Manager International, Virgin Atlantic

I have been fortunate enough to see the Hope Healing Home grow from an idea nearly two decades ago to the extraordinarily joyous and tangible message of love it is today. My sense of pride at the generosity and servitude of my family in bringing dignity and hope to the lives of these children cannot be expressed in words.

– **Adam Liaw,** Masterchef Australia 2010

It has been my privilege to watch as God has raised up Joyce and Robin to give life-saving care to many young orphans from across China. I know of nothing more central to our message of love or of greater importance to God, than to care for these that cannot care for themselves. You will discover how one couple fully sold out to God has made it possible for so many to live. A modern-day miracle of God using His people to change the world!

– **Jon Davis,** Lead Pastor, Beijing International Christian Fellowship

Liz Gifford's compelling account of how a family gave up their comfortable, expatriate life in China to take sick and abandoned orphans into their home is both moving and challenging. In telling how hundreds of China's most neglected children have been rescued from oblivion, the author remains lucid and unsentimental, letting the stories speak clearly for themselves. *The House of Hope* is what every reader longs for: a great story well told.

– **Rhidian Brook,** broadcaster and author

One of the greatest blessings of my work in China has been meeting Joyce and Robin Hill and getting to see through them what it means to be God's hands and feet in the world. They have shown me so clearly that until a child draws their last breath, we must do everything in our power to help them know love. Each and every day, through their tireless efforts, a true story of hope is being written for children who would otherwise be forgotten.

– Amy Eldridge, Executive Director, Love Without Boundaries Foundation

The reality of God's love explains how Rob and Joyce can so love the sick orphans of China! They have given their lives to care for each new arrival, as their very own, that each one may have life and be loved. New Hope Foundation is the "aroma of Christ".

– Sally Allred Lockett, Founder and Director, Portion for Orphans

The House of Hope

God's love for the abandoned orphans of China

Elisabeth Gifford

MONARCH
BOOKS

Oxford, UK, and Grand Rapids, Michigan, USA

First published in the UK in 2011 by Monarch Books
(a publishing imprint of Lion Hudson plc)
Wilkinson House, Jordan Hill Road, Oxford OX2 8DR, England
Tel: +44 (0)1865 302750 Fax: +44 (0)1865 302757
Email: monarch@lionhudson.com
www.lionhudson.com

ISBN 978 0 85721 059 3 (print)
ISBN 978 0 85721 146 0 (epub)
ISBN 978 0 85721 145 3 (Kindle)
ISBN 978 0 85721 147 7 (PDF)

Distributed by:
UK: Marston Book Services, PO Box 269, Abingdon, Oxon, OX14 4YN
USA: Kregel Publications, PO Box 2607, Grand Rapids, Michigan 49501

The text paper used in this book has been made from wood independently certified as having come from sustainable forests.

British Library Cataloguing Data
A catalogue record for this book is available from the British Library.

Printed and bound in Great Britain by Clays Ltd, St Ives plc.

Contents

Acknowledgments

It was a huge joy to spend time with the Hills and the babies at New Hope. Joyce and Robin were very generous in their hospitality, interview time and access to past newsletters. We took the decision to keep as close as possible to the words of all the interviewees. These stories need no embellishments. Huge thanks also to the many people who rushed to share their stories of Joyce and Robin's work, many of whom were running amazing support ministries for children in their own right – Amy Eldridge, Steven, Mary Beth and Emily Chapman, Delphine and Guillaume Gauvain of Bethel, and Dr Ngan, to name but a few. Thanks too to exceptional people like Simon Wu, and the staff of New Hope including Linda, Marsha, Xiao Jun, Rose, Mikey and Dr Zhai. Very many thanks, also, for the generous contributions of stories, Skype interviews and photographs from adoptive parents. It was a real privilege to share in so much happiness.

Thank you to Toby and Jing Littlewood who conceived of and facilitated this book, to Rhidian and Nicola Brook-Sulman for editorial advice, and to Frances Grant for copy-editing. Very sincere thanks also to Alan Dixon for copyright advice, to Josh Gifford for cover photography and to Tony Collins and Jenny Ward of Monarch for bringing this story to publication.

* * *

Elisabeth Gifford lives in Kingston and teaches children with dyslexia. She has written articles on literacy for the *Times*

Educational and *Independent* newspapers. She holds an MA in Creative Writing from the course run by Sir Andrew Motion at Royal Holloway University, London.

Foreword

The first time Mary Beth and I visited Robin and Joyce Hill in 2005, we immediately fell in love with the children and the way things were being done.

A year later we visited Joyce again, and she let Mary Beth go with her to see the new unit they were opening in an orphanage in central China. She told us that the orphanage was going to let her have the fifth floor to help the sickest children there.

We had already adopted three daughters from China by then, so we had seen the needs, but Mary Beth and I had never seen such devastating levels of need before. When Joyce explained how she was going to help those terminally ill children who were going to pass away – and help them to live their last days with dignity and love –then we knew that we had to do whatever we could to help Robin and Joyce carry out their work in China.

A year later we came back. We got to see how many of those same very sick children had survived. They had been given medical help and were thriving and being cared for – and we especially loved watching how Joyce really cares for all children as if they are VIPs. Some of them were well enough to go forward for adoption into families. It was so rewarding to see how many dying children were being rescued, loved and given a future.

Since then we have had the wonderful privilege of being a part of building the new home in Luoyang, Maria's Big House of Hope – named in honor and memory of our daughter Maria, who was a "special needs" orphan from China. We had the chance to spend a couple of days there in the first week it opened in the summer of 2009. We saw two little ones arrive who were so ill that they could only be loved and comforted as they passed away. We also saw many children who would one day be well enough to be adopted into their own families. It was such a privilege to be there.

Nine years ago, after we had adopted our own three daughters from China, Mary Beth and I began dreaming of some way to help some of the needy children we had seen there. Partnering with Joyce and Robin has meant that that dream has become a reality.

I love the quality of the work that the Hills do... and the results of their wonderful work in China have been nothing short of amazing. To date, they have cared for over 1,000 babies.

We as a family have come to realize that God truly loves orphans. Every time we do something to make their lives better, I believe He is there smiling and singing. You don't even have to say much – just "show up" and, as James 1:27 reminds us, "pure and true religion" will happen.

Robin and Joyce have changed the lives of many children, and I can say from experience that if you get involved with them, you will be changed as well.

Steven Curtis Chapman

Introduction

In November 1998, Rob and I clearly heard the call of God on our lives for the specific purpose of remaining in China and taking sick, disabled and abandoned children into our home; to love them and care for them as if they were our own, to treat their physical illnesses, and to heal the hurt in their hearts.

On 1 April 1999 (God does have a sense of humour!) we moved out to a small village and began to take children into our home. We thought we would be caring for just a few children, but to date Robin and I have taken in and cared for over 1,000 medically needy children. This may be a drop in the bucket compared to the needs out there, but every child has received our love and the best medical care we can provide. Many lives have been saved and many children now have "forever families". Many lives of those around the children have been touched and changed.

Since we set up that first baby's cot in our dining room, God's hand in providing for us has been nothing short of miraculous. As our organization grows, our desire is to keep on providing the children with the best care possible, always with the same standard of facilities that we would provide for our own children.

There have been difficult times, but God held us in His arms when we were suffering and He has not once failed us. We feel personally honoured to have experienced these past few years. This is His work and His children whom we care for.

So many people have encouraged and supported the home in every possible way. God bless you all. We pray that you will ceaselessly strive to walk with our Father in the plan that He has for your lives.

Let nothing deter you from serving Him.

Joyce and Robin Hill

1

The overnight train to Beijing

When my father and my mother forsake me, then the
LORD will take me up.

PSALM 27:10 (KJV)

In September 2003 a woman boarded the overnight train to Beijing carrying a newborn baby. The baby was extremely sick. She laid the little boy on her sleeper platform and curled herself alongside him. The other five people in the carriage had not been pleased to see a baby, but for a newborn he was strangely quiet. The woman put her hand in front of the baby's face to check that he was still breathing and hoped he would last until the train pulled in at Beijing Station in the morning. There, a second woman would be waiting to rush the baby straight to a hospital.

The baby took some sips of water, but was no longer feeding. Any milk made him gag. If you got close, the baby's breath was starting to have a sour, rotting smell, and his stomach was tight and distended. The woman could not sleep that night. Sometimes she put her hand on his chest to check that he was still alive. Once, she changed his diaper. It was damp, but not dirty. Since he had been born four days ago, this baby had not yet passed any meconium or waste matter. His diaper was never dirty. He had been born with a rare condition where there is no opening to the bowel. Soon he would begin to die as his digestive system began to back up. In such a tiny baby, this could happen very fast. Left to run its course, it was an agonizing death.

His birth parents had left the baby on the streets. It is hard to understand the kind of desperation that could drive parents to abandon their own child. Probably, they were too poor to be able to pay for hospital bills. Certainly they would not know that anything could be done to cure their baby's condition.

The very worst curse that you can give a Chinese father is to wish his son will be born with no anus, as this would mean not only the death of his precious son and heir but also the loss of the person who would continue to worship and pray for the family ancestors. Also, there are deep superstitions in rural China around dying children: in some areas, families still believe that the death of a child curses the house.

Perhaps both parents agreed to abandon the child. Perhaps the father took him while the mother slept. But during the night the baby was left on the streets of a town in Northern China. It was September, and the weather was still warm. By morning, he was found and taken to a Children's Welfare Institute. The staff wrapped him and left him, knowing that he would die.

The director of the baby's CWI happened to be visiting Robin and Joyce Hill at their new foster home in Beijing. Rob showed the director into the busy nurseries, with their active and healthy babies, and showed him the board with rows and rows of baby photos, explaining the different surgeries and medical care that had been arranged to save the children's lives. One little boy, called Gene, had been born without an opening to his bowel but had been given emergency surgery to save his life. The director looked puzzled.

"We have a baby with that condition," he said, "but we don't expect him to live very long."

"We can help him," Rob said, "if you can just get him here."

The director telephoned back to his Children's Welfare Institute. Within hours, the child was on the night train, accompanied by one of the CWI nannies, and within days a network of people had drawn together to try to save the life of this fragile child; funds were already coming in from places as far apart as Singapore and Tennessee to pay for the further surgeries needed after this emergency colostomy to restore the baby to complete health. It would take the effort of many people from around the world to bring together the skills, the funds and the will needed to form the net that would save this child's life. In some ways, it seemed an effort totally disproportionate to the size of this tiny, dying baby.

Far away on the other side of the world, another woman turned over in her sleep. It was getting colder now that it was September and she pulled the blankets up higher. Recently she had been restless and finding it hard to sleep. A short while ago she had applied to adopt a baby in China.

At Beijing Station, Marsha, a worker from Hope Foster Home, was waiting to take the baby from the CWI nanny. Joyce had briefed Marsha on the baby's condition and so she knew that she needed to get him over to the hospital fast. When she took him from the nanny's arms she saw a beautiful baby with a shock of black hair, but the child was very dehydrated and emaciated. She managed to get a taxi and watched anxiously as the driver negotiated the streams of Beijing traffic. The baby urgently needed to be put on a drip, as he would no longer take even a mouthful of water.

As a Beijinger, Marsha knew her way around the local hospitals and how things worked. She insisted on seeing a doctor quickly in spite of the queues of people already waiting. The doctor examined the child. He was surprised to hear that this was not Marsha's child, but an infant she had only just met. He was also surprised to see such a rare case present itself at the hospital. He agreed to arrange surgery urgently.

Marsha rang the office at Hope Foster Home and explained to Joyce Hill that the baby was doing as well as could be expected. He was on a drip and surgery was scheduled for the next day. Joyce told her a nanny would be arriving at the hospital soon who would stay with the baby in hospital while he recovered from surgery. She would be the baby's own nanny and would care for the child over the next two or three years while he lived at Hope Foster Home and underwent the second and third operations needed to complete his recovery.

Joyce Hill added the baby's name to the board of pictures in her office: photos of so many babies, once given up as hopeless cases but now getting the medical care they needed to be healed. To the right-hand side was a board of older babies and toddlers, bonny and healthy, with small stickers on the corner of each photo. These babies were now adopted and living with their new families.

Some of the newly arrived babies still looked very thin and unwell in their little pictures. Some of the new babies, in spite of every effort, would not make it. But all the babies would get the best possible care that could be arranged medically, and the love of their nannies and foster parents.

Again and again, people asked the Hills why they put so much effort and time into these unwanted and sickly babies, sometimes against the odds.

"I think God is painting a picture," Rob explains, "of how

God wants these babies to be treated; of how much He cares for even the most unwanted and, to human eyes, worthless among us. I think He is showing us that He wants to give the best care to those we consider the least. How much He cares for all of us."

Robin and Joyce Hill started off with one cot in the family dining room to care for one child. Since then they have cared for hundreds of sick and abandoned babies, working alongside several CWIs in China. Many lives have been saved, and many abandoned children have gone on to new lives with adopted families. Children who have been terminally sick have been cared for with love and have been able to die peacefully and with the best possible pain relief and care.

As well as their foster home in Beijing, the Hills have recently built a 150-bed unit, in partnership with the Show Hope organization, to care for children with a range of medical needs. The Hills now have four palliative care units for babies who are not expected to live, but where many of the children recover against all odds. They continue to take in sick children from near Beijing and from all parts of China, from as far south as Hainan Island and as far west as Urumqi.

Since they began in 2000, their work has expanded and they have met and begun to work alongside other people and organizations that have the same vision to help sick and abandoned children in China.

But there are still many needs to be met, and at present several areas in China are asking for the Hills to expand their help into new places. Sometimes, in a country of 1.3 billion people, the problems seem so vast that one might be tempted to feel hopeless and walk away. But the Hills always quote the starfish story:

*Hundreds of stranded starfish were dying along a beach,
and an old man was slowly throwing them back into the
sea one by one. Someone came along and pointed out
that his task was hopeless and told him, "It won't make
any difference, there are too many for you to save them."
But the old man held up a starfish and said, "It makes a
difference to this one," and then threw it back in the sea.*

It is impossible to meet the Hills and hear their story without asking questions about how you live your own life.

* * *

Robin and Joyce Hill are quite clear that it was never part of their life plan to stay in China and open a foster home for sick and disabled children. They were living in China and enjoying a comfortable expatriate lifestyle when their local church organized a visit to a children's home and Joyce and Robin went along. They took toys and diapers, and looked forward to an enjoyable day playing with the children.

But what happened during that day changed the course of their lives. Joyce said, "It was a heartbreaking experience for me to see the children's needs. I felt that we were just going there as rich expatriate people and bringing a few toys and diapers, but then we were coming away, and nothing was really going to happen to change those children's lives. The people we were with had been there before, and they were playing and laughing with the older children. But Robin and I spent our time with the younger babies and were just devastated by the conditions they lived in; we were crying the whole time.

"I think God put a burden on us that day. When Rob and I

came out we stood at the Children's Welfare Institute gates and we prayed. We prayed that we did not want to come back unless we could make a real difference to these babies' lives."

For the next four years, Robin and Joyce tried to find a way to make a material difference to the children's lives. Through his company, Rob offered help, but he was told that there were no orphans in need. No doors opened for them to be able to do anything to make a difference. Over time, the memory got pushed down. Joyce and Rob continued with their life as before, but they were never able to completely forget the needs that they had seen that day.

In 1998, Rob's four-year posting in China with his Swedish engineering company was coming to an end and it was time to move on to a new assignment. The Hills had decided that they wanted to move from China.

2 November was Rob's fiftieth birthday. As he shaved in front of the mirror that morning he was in thoughtful mood. He found himself praying. "Lord, there has got to be more to life than tungsten carbide and balance sheets and selling stuff to people to make a profit. There's got to be more to life than this."

A few days later, some friends invited Robin and Joyce to a meeting about a possible local project. The Hills had been part-owners of a small factory producing refrigerator magnets that aimed to raise funds to support community projects around Beijing. Joyce had been involved in running the Beijing sales office. Now, a piece of land nearby had become available where it would be possible to build a permanent community centre, and the people involved were going to discuss how it could best be put to use. Robin and Joyce knew that they would be leaving China but they went along to the meeting to offer any input they might have. Various ideas were discussed and Robin was pitching in with plenty of suggestions, but Joyce was strangely quiet. She sat through the meeting without saying a word.

She still did not speak as they left the meeting. They walked downstairs and got into the car ready to drive back home. Robin was surprised as Joyce sat next to him in silence. This was not her usual style.

"Well, what did you think of that?" he asked her finally.

She looked over at him and said, "I would like to ask our friends if we can use a third of the land. I think we should build our own home there and build a foster home for sick and unwanted babies. Rob, I think God is asking us to get into a river and I don't know where we are going to end up, but I think we should get in and we should just go with it. We have this opportunity to take in sick babies, and I think we are being asked to stay in China – to stay here permanently."

Robin stared at Joyce, speechless. He felt like a thunderclap had just hit him. He and Joyce found themselves sitting in the car, with tears streaming down their faces. It was a complete shock to both of them. Until that moment, neither of them had had any plans to stay, and certainly no plans to start a foster home.

Rob said later, "It was like God was sitting there saying, 'There, that's what I'm asking you. Do you want to do it?' And there was a sense that this was going to be something different, a real fun, rollercoaster ride – and that He was going to be with us. It wasn't like God was saying in capital letters, 'I WANT YOU TO GIVE YOUR LIVES TO ORPHANS.' It was more a sense that God was saying, 'This is really going to be different, and I am going to be with you.'"

Rob had worked for Sandvik for over twenty years, and during that time he'd been promoted to senior management and was set for a good retirement through the company. But in the space of two weeks, everything changed. He resigned from his company and he and Joyce decided to stay in China permanently and open a home for sick and unwanted babies.

2

Early years

For He has not ignored the suffering of the needy; He has not turned and walked away, He has listened to their cries for help.

PSALM 22:24 (NLT)

When you visit Joyce and Robin Hill at the New Hope Healing Home, you can't help noticing how happily and confidently the children run up to Joyce for a cuddle or to say hello. Clearly Joyce has a warm way with children, and yet she herself comes from a home where her mother was cold and hard-pressed as a parent, and where her own father was absent.

Joyce's grandfather, Edward Fredrick Holberton Edlin, was a prominent and well-loved lawyer in the British community in Singapore. But at the end of the First World War, the community was shocked to hear that Edlin had committed suicide by cutting his own throat, leaving Joyce's grandmother to raise eight children. The eldest five were at boarding-school in Britain, but Joyce's father and his younger siblings, Sydney and Topsy, would have been there at Endsleigh, the family estate, on the day that the body was found. Joyce's father, Edward Cecil, was only nine years old at the time.

The Second World War broke out some twenty years later. All

the Edlins' property was confiscated by the Japanese, or disappeared in smoke and flames on a bright blue day in February, when Singapore fell to General Yamashita. No one in Singapore was expecting an attack from the north, but the Japanese quietly made their way through the Malay jungle. Large numbers of Japanese soldiers rode down through Malaya in convoys of bicycles which could be easily hidden in the jungle. Hence this troop movement went undetected. The island of Singapore was astonished to find itself defeated, the harbour in flames and the red sunburst flags of General Yamashita fluttering against the blue February sky. Joyce's father and uncle were members of the Home Guard. Along with the 3,000 other British and Australian civilians, they were interned in Changi prison camp for the duration of the war, where food was inadequate and conditions were difficult.

Joyce's father, Edward, decided to stay in Singapore when the war ended, even though the infrastructure of the island was badly damaged. Although the Edlins had lost all their Singapore property, Edward still inherited considerable family wealth. Shortly after coming out of the prison camp, he met a young woman called Lucienne with striking looks that came from her French Indonesian ancestry. She was twenty years old – half Edward's age. They married and soon had a baby boy called Michael Peter; two years later Marguerette Joyce was born.

Edward's nerves and prospects did not survive the setbacks of the war years. He was unable to cope with the responsibilities of a young family. Beautifully turned out, and with impeccable manners, he left the house each day to spend a little more of the family's income on drink and gambling in various clubs. He became an alcoholic. Addicted to gambling on horses, he lost almost all of his fortune. But he never lost his manners as a quiet gentleman, and Joyce remembers her father at this time as a charming but hopeless drunk.

Joyce's mother could see that it was only a matter of time before there would be nothing left to pay for an education for the children. Lucienne was in her early twenties, but she found herself carrying all the responsibilities of raising two small children. The cooks, butlers, maids and governesses left after not being paid for many months. Lucienne brought her own mother in from Indonesia to care for the children while she went out to work at three different jobs to keep the family afloat. When Joyce was five and her brother Peter was seven, their mother finally divorced their father, and moved to Kota Bharu in the north-east of Malaysia, where she found a better job and the chance to try to start afresh. She took her mother and the children to live there, and apart from one time many years later, Joyce never saw her father again.

Lucienne was now the family breadwinner. They did not have much to live on, but her salary was enough to pay the rent on a village house and they had enough to eat. But Lucienne was still only in her late twenties, independent and strikingly beautiful. While working in Kota Bharu she met a well-respected anthropologist who worked for the Malay government as Commissioner of Aborigines. He came from an Austro-Hungarian background and carried himself like an officer. When Joyce was eight, her mother remarried and it must have seemed that the family would be able to enjoy a secure and settled life. However, it was not to be a happy outcome.

Unknown to her mother, Joyce's stepfather was also an alcoholic. But unlike her own father, he was a violent alcoholic. Joyce watched in horror as he regularly beat her mother with the walking-stick that he kept in the house. Joyce had to see this happening time and time again over many years.

There was no way of predicting his state of mind, and the house was always in a state of tension. Her stepfather drank secretly in his bedroom, and would suddenly appear in a drunken rage. He insisted that Joyce's mother dine formally with him each evening, and had liveried servants waiting at the table. If the dinner was not to his liking, then he would turn over the table and the beatings would start.

Joyce, her brother and grandmother ate rice and salt with the servants in the kitchen. Her grandmother did her best to make sure that the children ate enough and were dressed adequately, but no money was allocated for the children's clothes. The grandmother would have to beg her daughter to buy new uniforms for the children to go to school, insisting that one more washing would reduce their clothes to shreds.

For the children it felt like a harsh lesson in being unwanted and abandoned. Joyce's Indonesian grandmother had never received an education and could not read or write. In her culture, females were regarded as having little value. For Joyce, the awareness that their mother had abandoned them in favour of placating her stepfather was compounded by her grandmother telling her that she was stupid and ugly.

Through the next seven years the violent situation at home continued. Joyce's stepfather kept a loaded gun in the house. At one point he attempted to shoot her brother while in a drunken rage. Joyce could not understand how her mother had divorced a gentle wastrel of a drunk, her own father, and yet would not leave her stepfather, a dangerous and terrible man. Her mother had her own job, she owned her own home, and yet she could not leave him.

Joyce was now fifteen and found that her stepfather was beginning to behave towards her in an unhealthy and frightening way. Joyce's mother immediately sent her away to a convent boarding-school. To Joyce it seemed as if she was being blamed for causing the problems between her parents. It felt as if she was not wanted.

As she packed to leave, Joyce could not remember any hugs or kisses from her mother. She knew that her mother did not consider hugs and warmth as being vital to her children' welfare. All Lucienne's strength as a mother was channelled into making sure her own daughter grew up to be independent, to learn to rely on no one. She always insisted the children worked hard at school and told Joyce, "You have to train to be a doctor, because then, if your husband leaves you, you'll be able to look after your children."

Joyce had to leave behind the small zoo of waifs and strays that she had collected. She was notorious for bringing home stray cats and dogs, and over the years, her stepfather had brought home several exotic baby animals from the Malayan jungle and given them to Joyce. As Commissioner of Aborigines in Malaysia, he often visited villages in the jungle where people hunted bush meat such as small bears or monkeys. They were sometimes left with a pup or cub, and would then present it to the Commissioner. So Joyce found herself caring for a range of little creatures.

By the time she was nineteen, she had gained a scholarship to medical college in Kuala Lumpur. At the end of the first year in medical school she needed to pass in three papers to be able to continue into the second year. Failing those exams would mean not only a summer spent cramming but also the possibility of being thrown off the course if she did not pass the retake. But Joyce was finding it increasingly difficult to concentrate on her work. She was constantly worrying about her mother and the situation at home. When the end-of-year exam results came out, she was shattered to find that she had failed in all three papers.

Joyce was desperate. If she could not study hard enough to pass the papers in a year, then what chance did she have to pass her retakes in just two months? Perhaps she could cram for one paper, but not all three!

Then she got a call to go up to the Dean's office. This was always a grave matter; it meant that you had done something seriously wrong and could end in expulsion. Joyce knocked on his door and went in, expecting to be reprimanded. She stood in floods of tears in front of the Dean, unable to say anything, or to explain her failure.

The Dean waited until she had stopped sobbing, then spoke to her firmly.

"Joyce," he said, "stop crying now and look at me. What you have to do is put your family out of your mind. For the next two months, your family does not exist. It's just you and the exams."

Joyce was too stunned to say anything. Her stepfather, who by this time taught sociology at the university, had always put on a good front as a sober and respectable academic: no one knew about his drinking and his secret home life. But somehow the Dean did know. For the first time, Joyce did not feel so alone. She nodded and went away to work as hard as she could over the summer months.

When she came out of the exam room, she walked through Kuala Lumpur feeling exhausted. She had worked as hard as she could. For some reason she found herself going into a church and sitting down in the quiet building. Then she did something that she did not usually do; she started talking to God.

She said, "I have done all that I can. Now it is up to you, God. If you want me to be a doctor, then I will pass, and if you don't, then I won't pass. I put my life in your hands. I will accept what you want me to do."

When the results came out Joyce was amazed to see that she had passed in all three papers.

She says that after that prayer in the church, something changed for her. Being a doctor was no longer just about finding a way to earn an independent living as a woman in an insecure world. Joyce began to feel liberated into a great sense of compassion for the patients she was learning to care for.

Towards the end of her training, she came onto the ward and found the nurses standing round the cot of one of the babies. The baby's mother had slipped out in the night because the child had a rare blood disorder and would never live beyond the age of twelve. The little girl was beautiful, and it was hard to see why her parents would not want her. Joyce hated to think that the baby would have to be sent to the local orphanage.

So she went home that evening and announced to her mother that she was going to adopt the baby. Her mother was horrified. "You're absolutely crazy!" she argued with her. "You have no job. You have no husband. What are you doing?"

In the end Joyce conceded that she was not capable of looking after a child, but she never forget that baby, or the awful thought that when they heard the diagnosis, the parents had said to themselves, "We don't want her."

After graduating and starting work as a doctor, Joyce met and married a fellow student of Chinese ancestry. They had two little boys, but as Joyce had qualified through a government scholarship, she was contractually obliged to work long hours in the local hospital on Penang island in Malaysia, sometimes not returning home for three days. Her mother-in-law and maids cared for the boys. But Joyce was not happy. She desperately wanted to be able to spend more time with her children.

When they moved to Australia, Joyce's third child was born,

a little girl. Having a baby girl made Joyce question how she was going to bring up a daughter. Would she fall into the same cold habits as her own mother? Joyce said, "I was determined I was not going to treat her the same way that my mother treated me."

Joyce was determined to be the mother she wanted to be to Amber. "Every time I went to criticize her, I checked myself, because I thought, 'That's what your mother would have said to you.' I had to change the way I spoke to her, I had to force myself to hold her and hug her. I fed her for about a year and a half, and that helped. We made a very close bond. I could see now how a mother could be, and I had to take this picture that I had in my head, and be determined to show it. Because I think it is in you, to be a good parent, but you have to decide how you show it. Are you going to be hard or soft? Are you going to be criticizing all the time, telling them how to do things all the time as they grow up? – Even though it can sometimes mean having to let them go and make their own mistakes when they are older."

When her contract to repay her college fees to the government was ended, Joyce decided to start up her own practice so that she could take the children to work with her until they were old enough to go to school. This took some getting used to for her mother-in-law, as in Chinese culture it is traditionally the mother-in-law who is in charge of the grandchildren's upbringing. At first her mother-in-law was angry, but as things settled down, she and Joyce developed a warm and long-lasting relationship.

Joyce's small doctor's practice overlooked the long, unspoiled beaches of the Australian coast. Amber grew up in the little beach clinic and Joyce was able to be there when Amber started learning to walk and read. Joyce felt sad about the time that she had missed out on with the two boys while they were tiny, but she was now making sure that she used her days to build strong bonds with all her children.

The practice was going well, and life in Australia in the early 1980s was relaxed and pleasant. However, Joyce now had to accept that the man she had married was not going to remain her life partner. Their lives and values had taken different paths. They separated and divorced amicably and Joyce carried on working at the beach practice and committed herself to bringing up the children on her own.

3

Living by faith

Faith is being sure of what we hope for. It is being certain of what we do not see.

HEBREWS 11:1

One morning, a lady came into the surgery and, while she was seeing Joyce, began talking about the difficulties she was having in her marriage. Joyce always wanted to do something practical to help people: their children were about the same age and knew each other, so Joyce offered to have her children to stay over for the weekend.

"You and your husband could go away for a couple of days and try and sort things out," she suggested.

But sadly, when the couple came to pick the children up at the end of the weekend, things were no better. She and her husband Robin thanked Joyce for looking after the kids, and Joyce closed the door, disappointed to hear that she had not been able to help.

Some months later, Joyce recognized Robin when she saw him waiting in the surgery with his daughter. After Joyce had taken care of the little girl's sore throat, she asked him how he and his wife were getting on.

Robin looked uncomfortable. "My wife's been gone a while

now," he said. "She went to live in New Zealand with somebody else."

Joyce felt sorry for Robin. He was evidently working very hard to look after his three children and hold down a full-time job, but was finding life very tough. Joyce and her receptionist hatched a plot to try and find him a suitable new partner, by setting him up with a few well-chosen blind dates.

None of the blind dates seemed to work out, but in the process Joyce and Robin became good friends. Robin began to realize that the reason none of the dates seemed to be right was because he was falling in love with Joyce. Robin says, "I was always amazed that this doctor had been willing to get personally involved to the point that she would offer to babysit someone's kids. That always really impressed me about Joyce."

And Joyce began to realize that instead of helping Robin sort his life out, she was beginning to rely on his support. Whenever she had to deal with upsetting times as a doctor, he was the person she wanted to be with to talk through her day. She had fallen in love too.

So they decided to give dating a go – just the two of them, and their six children. At first Joyce would cook for Robin, and then go home and cook for her own family. Then they tried eating together with all their six children, taking it in turns to eat at each house.

After a while, Robin proposed. "Well, logistically, it was far simpler to just get married," he jokes.

There were many things to sort out and negotiate in combining two established families and lifestyles, as well as two careers and their own approaches to church and faith. They joined a small Uniting Church together, and shortly after they were married Joyce was baptized. The first thing she said to Rob after the baptism took place was, "I feel like I've just come home."

However, Robin had not always been so keen on church. As a child growing up in the English industrial Midlands, it was something he did not "get".

Rob's mother had walked out on he and his father while Rob was still small. Over time he found himself not only doing the cooking for his father, and living a latchkey lifestyle, but trying to cheer his dad up, since he had never been able to get over the hurt of his wife leaving. "In some ways," said Rob, "I stepped into the role of the parent. I was always trying to comfort Dad because I could see that he was hurting after Mum left. So I didn't grow up with a Dad as such – someone who would take you out to football or fishing. His whole life revolved around going to church and doing Bible studies."

Rob had his own problems to contend with. Without realizing the name of the problem, Rob was suffering from ADD (Attention Deficit Disorder), and he found formal study impossible. He hated school and, in spite of his best efforts, left with only two "O" levels. It was only years later, when one of his own children was given the diagnosis of ADD, that Rob realized it applied to him also. But by then, he could see that it had also given him many advantages, such as his energetic approach to life and his gift for innovative problem solving.

However, while he was a teenager, Rob was not interested in the church that took up his father's time. It seemed completely irrelevant to his interests, which centred around partying with his friends. When he was seventeen, Rob left home feeling little hope of sharing the closeness that a father and son long for.

It was only years later, when Rob moved to New Zealand with a young family of his own, that something changed. He says, "I was going for a job interview at a consultant guy's home up in the hills, and there was a church nearby. I wasn't a Christian or anything at that point, but I found myself standing outside that church having a conversation with God. I was thinking, 'This is a bit weird for me.' It was a very strange experience, because it was just like chatting to a friend, very clear."

Rob was willing to see if this "praying thing" had a positive effect, and went into the interview feeling quite sure that he was going to get the job. He did not get the job, but two years later, the Swedish engineering firm came back to Rob and offered him the same position that he had gone for that day. He stayed with Sandvik for many years.

Even though that interview was not immediately successful, Rob went home and found that a strange thing had happened. It was as if God had suddenly turned a switch on in Rob's internal hearing. God was there.

A few days later, Rob was handed an evangelistic newspaper called *Living Waters,* produced by some young people in New Zealand. Rob felt embarrassed about wanting to read such a thing, and had hidden it away from his wife, but one evening he got the paper out and debated about opening it up with her. It was a warm evening and he was trying to open a bottle of beer, but there was no sign of the bottle opener. "OK, God," he said. "If you want me to read the thing, then show me where the bottle opener is."

Rob doesn't remember if he ever found that bottle opener, but he started reading. He says, "I was struck by a reality in the testimonies of these people."

A while later he thought, "I've got to make a decision."

When he showed the magazine to his wife, she read it through and said, "We need to talk to somebody about this."

One of the people that Rob worked with helped to produce

the magazine, so, even though it was almost midnight, Rob rang Stuart and asked if he could come over and talk to him about this Jesus thing.

Stuart said, "Do you know what time it is?" but added wearily, "OK, then, you come on over here."

Stuart was a rough diamond who did not mince his words. He opened the door and greeted them with, "I'm not surprised you wanted to come over this late. My whole day's been ****."

In spite of this welcome, they went in and sat down. Stu said, "Oh my word, you are serious, aren't you?" because he could sense that the presence of the Lord was there. So Stu sat and shared. Then they prayed together and Rob and his wife made a decision to become Christians.

They both joined a small church with an elderly congregation and a traditional hymnbook, and they also went along to meetings at a young house church that encouraged speaking in tongues and prophecy, where the meetings were much less formal and sometimes seemed quite wild. It was confusing at times, but Rob felt that it was as if God was showing that there wasn't a right way or a wrong way. "It was as if we were being shown a balance, an interesting walk between the safe and the risky." It seemed to Rob that God was showing them that He was never as simple as people wanted Him to be.

But after moving to Australia, Rob and his wife drifted away from the church. Eventually she left Rob and went back to New Zealand with a new partner. Shattered, Rob tried to pick up the pieces of family life, desperately juggling work with looking after three children. He became part of a local church community again, and they helped out and supported him and his family.

Then one day, he had to take one of the girls to the doctor's surgery with a sore throat, and recognized the same doctor who had tried to help them out some months earlier.

* * *

When Joyce and Robin got married, Joyce had two boys and a girl, and Robin had two girls and a boy. If asked for advice about merging two families, Rob will say, "Pray." The older children were already teenagers. All the children were still hurting after the marriage break-ups. None of them had been expecting to end up with step-parents. It was a baptism of fire and a minefield.

Robin and Joyce found that they had very different parenting styles, but quickly realized that to make things work for the children, they needed to work together. It took a lot of negotiating as a couple, and they did not always agree with each other's approaches, but they made it clear to all the children that at the end of the day, they stood together. Rob had always been easy-going, whereas Joyce had always set very clear boundaries. Now his children were shocked to find that suddenly Dad meant what he said, and Joyce had to allow more adult rules for Rob's older children. But together, they let the children know that they were in agreement about wanting to make the new family dynamic work.

And then there were the sheer practical problems of running a house with six children. They had a boys' dorm and a girls' dorm and everyone had their own colour-coded towel: if there was a towel wet on the floor in the morning, then the lesson was, "If you don't hang your towel up, then fine, it doesn't dry: you'll have to use a wet towel." Joyce was to find that these skills and systems would come in very handy again one day.

Joyce began to talk about having another child, which initially mystified Rob since they already had six, but when Ryan arrived, all the children were united by sharing the same little brother.

4

A cot in the dining room

The important thing is this: To be able at any moment to sacrifice what we are for what we could become.

CHARLES DUBOIS

By the end of 1990 the five eldest children had left home for work or study. Rob and Joyce and their two youngest moved to Beijing so that Rob could take up the position of Coromant Division Manager for Sandvik.

At that time, Beijing was an unusual posting and all non-national workers were required to live in gated communities, so Robin and Joyce moved into an apartment in the Lido Hotel. It was a luxurious but somewhat enclosed lifestyle. Also it was hard work adapting to a new and very different country and learning to speak Mandarin. It helped that Joyce was familiar with Chinese culture.

During the summer the temperature in Beijing turns Mediterranean, and with a clubhouse, pool, tennis courts and restaurant on site, their life there often felt like a permanent holiday. Joyce found that after many hectic years of running her own practice and raising children, she suddenly had nothing to do. The children would wake up in the morning, order their breakfast from room service, grab their backpacks, take the lift down and then walk along the lane to the school. Joyce could visit the clubhouse for a swim, or perhaps go to the gym, but when she got back the apartment was clean and all the beds were made. She said, "I could have a bubble bath, or twiddle my thumbs. There was nothing to do. There were no libraries, and only so much TV you could watch."

Then Joyce got a phone call. An American medical group, called SOS, was expanding into Asia. Joyce jumped at the chance to work again, but stipulated that she needed to finish work in time to be home for the children each day.

What Joyce had not realized, however, was that SOS needed doctors with foreign passports who could be available at all hours to accompany medical evacuations. She found herself regularly collecting patients at the hospital in Beijing and taking them to the airport. The seats at the back of the plane would have to be removed to make room for a sick passenger and then Joyce would monitor the patient's drips and medical equipment until they arrived in America or Australia. But now she found that she was hardly seeing the children, so as soon as the practice was able to find more doctors to cover the work, she resigned.

Joyce decided to join a quilting group to help raise funds for the Christmas bazaar. Although she initially thought it was a somewhat ridiculous activity to cut up perfectly good cloth into pieces and then sew them all back together, she was soon a great devotee of the craft, producing beautiful quilts in large quantities.

It was strange to look back, several years later, and see how Joyce's skills in both medical evacuations and mass quilt production were to prove essential one day, in ways that Robin and Joyce could never have imagined as they went about their lives in the calm luxury of the Lido Hotel.

The Hills enjoyed attending the thriving international church in Beijing, and Joyce signed herself and Rob up to go on a day trip to visit a nearby Children's Welfare Institute. They came home from that trip shaken and determined to do something real to help the children they had seen there. They desperately wanted to do something practical, but all attempts to get involved in a meaningful way came to dead ends. Joyce and Robin accepted with sadness that that door was closed.

Rob was about to turn fifty and he and Joyce were busy making plans to leave China, when one morning they decided to go along to a meeting to discuss a piece of land that had become available for a new community project. They would be leaving soon, but at least they could offer their friends any input they might have.

The first hint that Rob got that something was about to change, was the way Joyce sat through the whole meeting in total silence. This was undoubtedly a first for her. As they sat in the car ready to go home, she was still silent. When Rob asked her what she thought, she dropped her bombshell.

Joyce's reply would change everything. She turned to Rob and said that she thought God was asking them to stay in China permanently and build a foster home on part of the community land. Then, they could start to take in sick and abandoned babies. It seemed, she said, as if they were being asked to step into a river, and although she had no idea where they would end up exactly, they could trust that it would take them to the right place.

As Joyce shared how she felt, Rob found that he understood exactly what she was saying. They both burst out crying. In the space of just a few sentences, the direction of their lives changed. They were going to stay in China and open their home to sick and abandoned babies.

There was no plan to stay before that moment. Rob says, "We

made the decision sitting there in the car that night. We didn't weigh it up. We didn't think, 'Can we afford this?' or 'What about our retirement?' The only thing we had a real sense of was that if we were going to make the decision to take a child into our own home, then we would do it as if they were our own children. And so that's how the decision was made, knowing that we might be looking after a child for the next eighteen years. This was not going to be a short-term thing for two or three years. We knew that we were going to be in it for the long run."

Robin and Joyce drove home to tell the children about their plans, worried that they would find such a radical change in their lifestyles a shock. But Amber and Ryan were as excited as their parents about their plans to stay in China and look after children who were sick and unwanted.

Joyce says, "Not once did the children complain about having to move out of the luxurious Lido complex into a small flat in a village near Beijing. Of course, they still carried on at the same school and kept the same friends, thanks to the support of Rob's company, and that really helped with the transition into a new life."

Rob knew that he would have to resign from Sandvik after twenty years of very satisfying work. He wondered what the CEO from Sweden would think of their plans. Everything was already set for Rob to leave China and take up a new post. When Rob's boss arrived at the Sandvik headquarters in Beijing, he sat down in Rob's office and asked if Rob had decided on Australia or another location.

Rob took a deep breath and said, "Why don't you offer me some kind of leaving package? Because we think we're going to stay here in China."

For the next half hour Rob outlined how they hoped to build the foster home and take in sick and abandoned babies. The CEO was shocked but very supportive. The company gave Rob a good package with half salary for the next twelve months and help to keep the children at the International School for another couple of years.

So on 31 December 1998, only two months after Rob had woken up on his fiftieth birthday and prayed, "God, there must be more to life than tungsten carbide and balance sheets," he resigned and ended twenty years of working for Sandvik.

Rob's friends in the office knew that he was a Christian and "a little bit strange", but the reaction when he said goodbye was unexpected, with people in the office very supportive and curious about their plans. But Rob was adamant that he and Joyce were not doing anything brave – it was simply something they were being asked to do. In fact, as far as retirement plans went, he was the first to point out that it was a rather silly thing to do.

The Hills did not have any plans for how they would support themselves financially, or how the new home would be funded. Rob had always been a conscientious provider for the family, but he now found that worries about having enough money seemed to be taken away. "I know it sounds like we just wandered away into the ministry like a couple of fairies," Rob says, "but all we knew was that God was asking us to do this, and that we could rely on Him. It was as if He just wrote it into our hearts: we could rely on Him."

But the next thing that happened amazed both Joyce and Robin. As they began to make plans to set up the home, friends from the church and the expatriate community began to come to them with the same response: "What can we do to help? How much do you need?"

The team running the community project gave the Hills permission to use part of the land to begin building the new foster home. So on 1 April, the Hills moved from the Lido apartment into a little village apartment while the new home was being built. They were leaving a smart, Westernized compound near Beijing, with plenty of modern shops and facilities, and moving into the same kind of basic apartment block that many Chinese families lived in, situated a long way out in a rural village. However, apartments were usually sold as a concrete shell, so Rob was able to install wooden floors and turn the flat into a very comfortable home. His friends teased him that he had turned their flat into a mini Lido Hotel. There was nothing that could be done about the plumbing, however. All the pipes in the building ran almost horizontally and unblocking the loo was a daily problem. Rob vowed that in their new home, all the plumbing would be correctly installed so that he would never need to use his plunger again!

Joyce was proud to see that both Amber and Ryan were happy to move to a two-bedroom apartment so small that there was only room for one person to stand in the kitchen and do the dishes. The apartment was also up five flights of stairs, with no lift, and there were many things that Joyce found exasperating. If she plugged in the Hoover at the same time as the microwave, then the electrical junction box would burst into flames and she would burst into tears – and wonder what on earth they were doing there.

But gradually Joyce adjusted to their new life. Having grown up in Malaysia, she had known poor times and also wealthy times. She thought of it all as just another adjustment in life.

Ryan loved the freedom of living in a village. Rob fixed up a small motorbike for him to ride around the village and he soon made friends with all the local children, and knew which shop sold the best firecrackers or sweets. The villagers named Ryan "Little Yellow Jumping Bean" because of his very blond hair and bouncy personality.

It was the children who began a campaign to take in the first baby. They took it in turns to keep up their request: "Oh Mum, go on, just one baby." Joyce pointed out that they had absolutely nowhere to put a baby until the new home was built. Where was the baby to go – in the dining room?

But after much prayer, the family decided that yes, they had already waited too long. So with great excitement Ryan and Amber helped to assemble a cot in the dining room, ready for their first new arrival.

5

Kaitlyn

What value has compassion that does not take its object in its arms?

ANTOINE DE SAINT-EXUPÉRY

Four years before Rob resigned his post and they moved into the Chinese village, he and Joyce had stood outside the gate of a Children's Welfare Institute and prayed that they would not go back there unless they could make a real difference to a child's life.

As Chinese New Year came round, the Hills went back to that same Children's Welfare Institute to attend a children's concert. By then, the director had got to know the Hills a little more and Joyce had explained how she wanted to help with difficult medical cases, and open their home to care for such children. The director had been out to visit their new project and liked what she saw of their plans. So while they were at the concert, Joyce and Robin took a deep breath and decided to let the director know that they were ready to take in their first child, a child who would be under six months old and who had a medical need that they could get fixed.

"We haven't opened fully yet," Joyce explained, "but we could take one baby into our own home."

"I do have a child who needs help," said the director. "She's got a big growth here." The director indicated the side of her neck.

She sent for the baby and one of the nannies brought back a little girl, about five months old. The baby couldn't turn her head because she had such large cystic growth on her shoulder.

Joyce immediately said, "We'd like to try and help her."

Kaitlyn was wrapped in a red blanket and the family stopped to have their photo taken, Robin carefully holding the little bundle and Amber and Ryan smiling widely, one on each side of baby Kaitlyn.

As Rob carried Kaitlyn down the steps of the CWI, he looked down at her round face staring out at the world inquisitively and thought, "We are going to make a real difference to the life of this little girl." It was hard to believe that they had stood on those steps and prayed to come back to that Institute only when they could make a real difference to a child, and now, after so many failed attempts, it really was happening. He felt humbled and amazed that he and Joyce had been given this opportunity to give the little girl a chance of full health.

Baby Kaitlyn had pink, chubby cheeks and was bright and intelligent, but when Joyce and Amber undressed her for her first bath, they both began to cry: the baby was skin and bone underneath her clothes. Her ribs were showing and she was very malnourished and hungry.

The first task was going to be to help her gain weight.

* * *

It was exciting to see the shell of their new home completed, and a team of local builders began working on the internal electrics and plumbing. Joyce and Robin were amazed to see that the building costs had all been met. They also had enough in the foster home fund for at least six months of running costs once they opened.

They approached the Government Civil Affairs departments to find out the best way to register the new foster home, but it soon became apparent that this was not going to be as simple as it first appeared. Robin found that the old adage, "It is better to ask for forgiveness than permission," sprang to mind a lot when working with the government agencies.

In the meanwhile, with the apartment dining room in use as a nursery, space was tighter than ever, but Robin and Joyce soon had two more children to take care of: Daniel was the fourth child of a local family, and the Hills had agreed to look after the baby until his own parents felt able to take him back; and Christie was a four-year-old girl from Luoyang in Henan province. She had had part of a large vascular growth removed from her chin and mouth, but needed extra care as the operation had left the skin weak and her lower lip had split in two. The remaining growth bled profusely after meals. Each time she ate, food got trapped in the ragged skin and needed syringing out. Joyce was touched to see how patiently Christie would wait with the little bowl under her chin until the job was done. She was waiting for her adoptive parents to come and pick her up, and the rest of the growth was going to be removed once she arrived in America. It would take many surgeries to close off the blood vessels, but in the meantime the Hills had been asked to help while the first surgery healed. Christie also had a slight speech difficulty and called herself Yaya, which soon became her nickname.

All the family pitched in to help with the childcare, but Joyce realized that they would need to start training nannies to help care for these babies. In the meantime, Xiao Jun, a graceful and sweet girl from the village, came in to help with the cleaning. But even as a cleaner, Xiao Jun drew the line at cleaning up after Yaya who was going through a stage of refusing to use her potty. When Yaya made yet another mess, Xiao Jun stood there and thought, "It is not my job to clean up the children." But then Robin came in, saw to the mess and swabbed down the floor.

Years later, when Xiao Jun was working at New Hope as staff manager, she told Joyce: "All the while I stood and watched in silence, and wondered why this foreign man, who gave up a well-paid job, would sacrifice so much for the sake of an 'ugly' Chinese orphan. He could have ordered me to clean it up, but he did not. What was it in this man's life that he saw these children as so deserving of such love? At that point I understood the love of Yesu for these children, not through words but through a simple, humble act."

Xiao Jun was to later become a key person in the life of the home, and one of the Chinese friends and co-workers that the Hills trust and rely on, through both happy times and hard times.

* * *

The Hills still often wondered if they were doing the right thing for Ryan and Amber. But one afternoon, as Robin and Ryan were riding into the village on their motorbikes, Ryan shouted across, "You know, Dad, I wouldn't go back to the Lido for anything." Robin smiled. It was good to know, he thought, that even though there was no longer anything fancy about where they were living, the children could be just as happy.

The village was typical of many rural villages in China, built around a dusty, grey crossroad of one-storey shops, festooned overhead with bunches of electrical cables running in all directions to telegraph poles or roofs. On most days the village square was filled with market stalls, each with a makeshift plastic canopy or large umbrella to give some shade, and piled high with mounds of knobbly vegetables from the nearby farms. Brushes, pots, plastic bowls and all manner of household goods queued up next to the stalls or were spread out neatly on squares of tarpaulin.

At the time, Beijing was beginning to fill up with smart new cars, but out in the countryside most people still rode bicycles. Enormous loads of boxes or mounds of cut bamboo leaves would mysteriously sail through the streets of the village, and on closer inspection there would turn out to be someone pedalling hard on a three-wheeler bike beneath the load. It was not unusual to see a wardrobe or other, equally large bits of furniture floating by on such a bike.

The paperwork needed for Christie's adoption and Kaitlyn's surgery was slowly moving forward. It was good to think of the time when they would have no health problems and people would be able to see how beautiful these children truly were. For the time being, though, both girls had disfigurements that made people stare when the Hills took them out.

Robin, who enjoyed cooking gourmet-style meals with fresh and inexpensive local produce, liked to do his shopping at the village market. The Halal meat stall was run by a local man who always entertained his customers with a line of loud comic patter, and he and Rob had become friends. One morning, the butcher was surprised to see the Hills arrive with a small baby in a buggy. He came out from behind the stall to have a better look, but when he saw a large growth bulging from the baby's shoulder he recoiled and was evidently distressed. He asked many questions about the baby and what the Hills were doing. So the Hills explained that she was their first foster child and that they were looking after her while they arranged for the cystic growth to be removed. He immediately began to tell everyone else around the stall in a loud voice what the Hills were doing.

They went home, a little taken aback by the butcher and his reactions.

As they were sitting down to their evening meal, the phone rang. It was another foreign couple living in the block. They said that they had a Chinese couple at their door, looking for the foreigners with the baby. "Shall we tell them where you live?" the friend said. Rob and Joyce agreed that it couldn't do any harm, but waited with some anxiety for their visitors.

There was a knock at the apartment door. Rob answered it to find the butcher and his wife standing on the doorstep. They came in and started unpacking bags of fruit, baby milk and a whole tableful of little treats for the children and the family.

Rob and Joyce were overwhelmed, even more so when the butcher and his wife explained that they wanted to come and say thank you, on behalf of all their community, for caring for this orphan child. Rob and Joyce felt very touched: in the Chinese culture the giving of food is of great significance, showing sincere love and respect for the recipient, something far more significant than the giving of a fruit basket or muffin basket in the West.

Rob was English and a Christian. The butcher was Chinese and a Muslim and yet, Rob thought, because they had a common concern of wanting to look after a child, all those cultural barriers counted for nothing. They were able to come together and communicate with no difficulty. Robin and Joyce were very encouraged by this support from the village, and the butcher became a good friend – the first of the many friendship links with the local people that the Hills and the foster home would come to value over the next few years.

The weather began to get warmer, and the cicadas began to tune up for their summer concert across the wide-open fields around Beijing. Out in the village square groups of men appeared sitting round picnic tables to play cards or *mah-jongg*, or whole families could be seen outside the family shop, resting on their haunches to have a chat, or to just watch the world go by, their washing hung out on coat hangers in a nearby tree. It became so hot and muggy in the afternoon that stallholders sometimes laid themselves out on the emptied stalls and had a long nap to the sound of the incessant cicadas.

It was also getting extremely hot and stuffy in the Hills' little flat. The children in particular found the heat difficult. So Robin managed to move them all into a larger apartment, and the best thing about the new place was that they now had air-conditioning, as a present from a couple at church – invaluable when the weather became so hot that they could no longer take the children outside for walks.

With the new home nearing completion, Joyce was able to start planning to move in. She and Robin decided that they needed one nanny for each two children, and also a good ratio of night nannies. If the children were to experience real family relationships, then their nannies would need to have enough time to bond with them. Joyce began to interview women from the village and found four excellent young women, all loving and responsible, who followed their new training with enthusiasm. The children would have various medical needs so Joyce also taught the nannies some basic nursing. She also hired cleaners and a cook to help in the daily running of the foster home and so allow enough time for her to concentrate on the medical side of the children's needs.

By the end of September, with everyone working like crazy, and donations of cots and towels arriving daily along with the teams of helpers, the new home was finally ready. The new babies' rooms were each painted a different colour, with coordinating patchwork quilts made by Joyce. In child-sized cupboards the baby clothes and towels also had colour-coded tags so that each child had his or her own personal things. The new bathrooms and kitchen looked so smart that some visitors expressed surprise that this was for abandoned orphaned children, in an area where many rural families did not expect to live in such a nice place.

But Robin and Joyce were adamant that the children were part of their family, and deserved all that they would want for their own children in terms of cleanliness and living conditions. One of the guiding principles, for the Hills, was that although the children had once been discarded and their medical problems had led them to be shunned, in God's eyes these children deserved the best.

6

The new home is ready

The biggest disease today is not leprosy or tuberculosis, but rather the feeling of being unwanted.

MOTHER TERESA

In October 2000, the Hills finally moved into Hope Foster Home.

Joyce and Robin got the babies settled into their cribs, sorted out Amber and Ryan's rooms, and then fell into their own bed surrounded by piles of cardboard boxes. But in spite of her messy room, Joyce felt completely happy: they had their own home in China. Tomorrow, she could get down to organizing the medical dressings and supplies in the new cupboards and finding out exactly where everything was. If Robin always had hundreds of ideas and plenty of energy to carry out the ones that were passed, then Joyce was the one who was always very organized and precise. Together, they balanced each other out to make a good team.

A few days after moving in, the Hills set out to collect the first new arrivals at Hope Foster Home: a boy with an extra thumb that could easily be removed, thus greatly increasing his chances of being put forward for adoption; and a little girl called Molly. She was only three months old, but Joyce could already see that she was very bright. Both babies had been abandoned on the street.

Molly had spina bifida and it would now be a race against time to fix up surgery to close the lower spine bulge before it began to affect her leg movement, so as soon as they were home Joyce began to search for doctors able to help. Although she was not a fan of computers, she found she was learning how to use email and internet searches very quickly so that she could contact specialist surgeons all over the world.

Both babies were going to need passports before they could travel overseas for surgery, but after many visits to their original CWI to get passports issued, the Hills came up against a brick wall. The director was already frustrated at not being able to issue a passport for Kaitlyn so, to solve at least one problem, she finally turned to Robin and said, "If you like this baby so much, why don't you adopt her?"

The Hills had loved little Kaitlyn from the first day they met her. With her sweet face and sunny personality, she was now walking and getting into mischief everywhere in the house. Robin and Joyce were prompted by the director's question to begin to hope that she might one day become their daughter and the eighth child in the Hill family. So after praying and considering this, they started along the long trail of necessary paperwork towards her adoption. It seemed endless, and frustratingly slow, but they were determined to get everything in place as soon as possible so that Kaitlyn could have the cyst removed before it grew any larger.

In the meantime, another baby arrived at Hope Foster Home. Amelia had been found abandoned on the street, and seemed to be about two months old. She was extremely malnourished and fragile and the immediate concern was to get more food into her so that she could grow stronger.

But Amelia refused to feed and cried incessantly because of

colic. Her nannies tried and tried but Amelia was now dangerously malnourished, so Joyce went back to broken nights, keeping the child by her bed and feeding the baby tiny amounts. It was a gruelling experience, to be waking up for night feeds at the age of fifty, but bit by bit Amelia put on weight, and eventually could take a full bottle, and then go happily down in her crib for a long nap. Gradually the baby's face began to fill out so that she looked like a baby rather than a little old person. Amelia was out of danger.

They also accepted baby Shaun, who was waiting for his adoptive parents to collect him; a little girl called Hannah, who was three months old and had an ear missing; and a tiny baby called Joshua, who was born prematurely and needed considerable extra care.

One year after they had set up that one cot in the dining-room, Joyce, Robin, Ryan and Amber celebrated Christmas with nine babies and their nannies. The babies had great fun opening presents from England and Beijing.

Other presents for the home that Christmas included a truckload of formula from the American Community Club, and a large quantity of toilet paper and cleaning products from one of the Chinese schools. The Hills were constantly amazed by how many people had come together, unprompted, to give time and money so that the children could get better and even, perhaps, be adopted one day. As Joyce and Robin looked around that Christmas, they realized that Hope Foster Home's every need had been met.

In January their first two children to be adopted left Hope Foster Home. For some time, Joyce had been showing photographs to Christie and Sean to introduce them to their new mummies and daddies, and help prepare them for their new lives in Virginia,

USA. It was a bittersweet day for everyone in the foster home, as Christie and Sean, dressed in their favourite clothes, and with their special things in little backpacks, stood together on the doorstep, ready to go back to their Institutes where their new families would collect them. As the children drove away for the last time, Joyce knew that although she was crying, she was very happy. The ultimate hope for every child at Hope Foster Home was that they would not only be healed, but one day also adopted by their own "forever family".

It was also time for Amber to leave to go to university. They were going to miss her terribly. She showed a real heart for taking care of children and always got involved with their day-to-day care. When, a few years later, Amber decided to study medicine, Joyce could not have been more proud of her.

All through January and into February, Joyce had been trying to find a surgeon able to operate on both Molly and Kaitlyn, but twenty different leads came to nothing. She was now waiting for a reply from a hospital in the USA.

In the meantime they had space to help two new babies, so Joyce, Robin and a volunteer called Joy drove to a nearby CWI. The hard thing was going to be deciding which babies to bring home, since so many had pressing medical needs.

The director there was a wonderful woman who did all she could to care for the children. She had been out to visit the Hills' foster home and was happy for Joyce to take some of her at-risk children in need of urgent medical care. She showed Joyce a baby of just four weeks called Megan, who had been left in the snow and brought in to the CWI by a policeman. Megan had frostbite, but Joyce was relieved to see that it had only mildly affected her toes and could easily be treated. She also agreed to take Sophie, who was very underweight and had a clubbed right foot, which

Joyce could treat in the home. Two babies for two beds.

And then she found Jordan, an eight-month-old little boy with a bladder that was only partially formed and lay open on his tummy like a small disc. This was a much more complicated operation, but Joyce felt that she could somehow find a surgeon to help Jordan. So she agreed to take all three.

But she had not reckoned on Rob. He and Joy had found a minute and premature baby called Shayna. They were really concerned for this dangerously thin child. Joy was already holding Shayna.

"We have to take her," Rob insisted.

"Stop," said Joyce. "Then that's it. After Shayna, we can't take any more."

But as Joy and Joyce went out through the door, happily chatting about having to employ another nanny pretty quickly, Rob caught up with Joyce and pulled her back.

"Joyce," he said, "come and look at this one. If we don't take her, she will die."

Rob showed her a little girl lying in a cot. She was called Claire and she was tiny for four months old. She was skin and bones with sunken cheeks and sores covering her face. The sores had spread inside her mouth so that she had stopped drinking. She was breathing in a shallow, dry way because of acute pneumonia, and when Joyce looked in her eyes, she could see that the child had given up the will to live.

Joyce began to cry. If they did not take her, Claire would certainly die.

So they took her. Five babies and two spare beds! It was so difficult to leave babies behind.

Already, it seemed, they needed to expand.

After a couple of weeks Claire was out of danger, but Sophie was still having a lot of feeding difficulties. She had weak swallowing muscles and every time she tried to swallow, the milk would go down into her chest and up her nose. Joyce knew that if the milk proteins settled in the lung tissue they would cause a degenerative acid reaction, so they began the many months of feeding Sophie through a tube. The nannies sweetly let Sophie suck on a comforter each time they fed her through the tube, so that the sensations of sucking and of her tummy filling up coordinated in Sophie's brain.

Joyce tried again and again to get a travel permit to take Sophie to a specialist in Hong Kong, but without success. In April they took her to a local hospital for further investigations and were amazed and relieved to find that by the time they got to the hospital, Sophie was finally able to feed well and independently. Joyce watched her drink a full eight ounces from a bottle with no difficulties. It was a wonderful feeling to know that Sophie was going to be well.

Claire, the little baby who had been so close to slipping away that they could not leave her behind, looked like a different child now that her sores had cleared and she was a normal weight. A family in Canada went on to adopt Claire and later sent photos back to Joyce of a lovely, healthy child who came top of her class.

But right now, Claire was sleeping in her cot under her new patchwork quilt, and Joyce was checking on all eleven babies with an overwhelming feeling of joy at seeing them healthy, happy and growing. In the stock room she noted that they were low on baby wipes and cereal, but marvelled again at how support seemed to come in from all sorts of groups. She wondered how many other babies had their diapers supplied by wives of the Defence Attachés.

While they were settling into the new home, and already seeing the need to expand, someone offered the Hills a very large sum of money to allow them to buy an adjacent piece of land and so extend the Home. This would mean that they could take in a total of eighty children. The generosity of the offer was overwhelming, but so was the awesome responsibility of caring for eighty children – caring for them as if they were their own children. And yet, as Joyce pointed out, considering the great need that existed, eighty children still seemed a drop in a bucket.

It was around this time that Robin and Joyce were told about an old man in the village. He had contacted some local friends and shared with them a dream he had had sixteen years earlier. The old Christian farmer explained that the plot of land was considered cursed in the village because many people had committed suicide there. Nobody wanted it. But in the dream he saw that God was going to change that place by blessing it. He dreamed that foreigners arrived and built a home for orphans there. In the morning he told his son, but his son did not believe him. Foreigners were unheard of in the villages. Building a home for orphans on a cursed piece of land? Not likely!

Joyce thought back sixteen years. She and Rob had only just met each other. Back then China was just another country on a map. They certainly had no plans to go there. But God had plans, and it was awesome and humbling to realize that she and Rob had been part of those plans, even though they knew nothing of it at the time.

With the offer of funds to expand, Robin and Joyce were certain about one thing. They knew that they could not do the next phase alone. So many people had been there to support them as they opened the home. All their needs in looking after the children had been met, every time. But caring for a total of eighty children seemed a very serious undertaking.

7

So many babies – how to get them help in time

Love anything and your heart will possibly be broken.
If you want to keep it intact… give it to no one. Wrap
it carefully with hobbies, and… luxuries… But in that
place of dark, motionless, airless safety… it will become
unbreakable, impenetrable, and irredeemable.

C. S. Lewis

Joyce was delighted when she finally heard back from a charitable organization in the USA, willing to operate on both Kaitlyn and Molly. Molly's swelling was growing, pulling tighter on the spinal nerves with an ever-increasing risk that the baby might lose the function in her legs and bladder. With the preliminaries at last complete, Joyce hurried to get their passports and papers stamped for America.

But then Joyce found out that she would not be allowed to travel out with the girls. Instead, an airline hostess would accompany them, and unknown volunteers – strangers to the children – would oversee them while they were in hospital. Joyce offered to pay for her own flight out so she could look after Kaitlyn and Molly, but the organization could not change the system.

Joyce did not see how she could hand the children over to complete strangers and let them go through frightening major surgery with no familiar faces, no familiar smells or voices. She could not let this happen to the girls. So Joyce firmly turned down their offer of help.

But the girls' passports were now stamped for America. She had no option but to find another American surgeon. Joyce urgently tried twenty different hospitals in the USA and finally received a reply from Dr Noel Tulipan, Professor of Neurological Surgery at Vanderbilt Hospital, Nashville. He had carried out foetal repairs on spina bifida cases. If anyone could save the function of Molly's legs, then he could. He also offered to arrange for surgery for Kaitlyn.

Joyce immediately replied to fix a date for the girls' surgery. But as she read through Dr Tulipan's email, she saw that there was another huge problem: even though the surgeon would make no personal charge, and the hospital was willing to reduce its fees, the cost of the surgery was going to be much more than they expected.

Rob was working in his office when Joyce walked in that morning. "I need $50,000 for Kaitlyn and Molly's surgery," she announced.

Rob looked at her in shock. "We don't have that much in the foster home bank account," he told her.

They sat together in silence.

"If these two little girls were both our own daughters, would you let me take $50,000 from our own savings?" asked Joyce.

"I know you have faith that God will provide for this," Rob told her, "but give me a chance to catch up here. I haven't quite got that much faith yet."

But since the day they decided to stay in China and open a

foster home, Robin and Joyce had made a commitment to treat all the children in their care as if they were their own.

Rob gave a sigh and said, "Go on then, take it from our account."

So two weeks later, Robin and Joyce boarded a plane carrying Kaitlyn and Molly, for the 7,000-mile journey to Nashville.

Dr Tulipan examined Kaitlyn. The lymph vessels in her neck were defective, causing a growing cystic bulge. It would be tricky surgery because it involved the delicate neck and shoulder area where many nerves and vessels lay, but Dr Tulipan reassured Joyce that Dr Pietsch would be able to completely remove the growth.

Molly's case, however, was very risky. The baby's spine was split open and a spur of ragged bone jutted out from one of the vertebrae. She was admitted for urgent surgery and Dr Tulipan carefully removed the bone spur, untethered her spinal cord and then sewed a tough, synthetic membrane over the spinal opening, covering it all over with a flap of skin. Molly's spinal structures could now grow normally.

When she came round everyone was thrilled to see that she had kept full movement in both her legs.

Kaitlyn was up and running around the hospital and getting to know everyone the very next day after surgery. Dr Tulipan declared that the only problem this baby had was being too full of beans.

As they left Vanderbilt Hospital holding two healed little girls, Robin and Joyce felt privileged to see how much everyone had cared about the children and had gone out of their way to help them. The hospital bills were also much less than expected at $35,000, and while the girls had been in hospital, funds had come in to cover all the remaining costs for their surgery.

When they got back to Beijing, Joyce and Robin were given

the news that Kaitlyn's adoption had been officially approved. She was now truly their daughter. In a month's time they would fly back home to Australia for a family vacation, and then Katie could meet her other five brothers and sisters.

But just before they set off, Joyce went to a CWI to offer to take another baby. She was shown Katherine, lying listlessly in her crib. She had a heart condition and was painfully thin, with blue lips. At ten months, she was older than most of the babies they took, and knowing that her treatment would be very costly, Joyce started to move away. But she was struck by a look in the child's eyes that made her turn back. Katherine's eyes seemed to say, "Am I not worth it?" Joyce knew the answer. She found herself weeping as she picked up the baby and took her home.

Joyce quickly got a response from a group in Israel called Save a Child's Heart. They would be sending a team out to China, so Joyce took Katherine for tests in Beijing and the results were telecommunicated to the surgeons in Israel. Katherine had an extensive hole in her heart and the main artery to the lungs was closed; a very small blood vessel in its place was all that was keeping her alive. The surgeons told Joyce that Katherine's case was too complicated for them to operate upon.

But Joyce immediately began a new search for someone who was willing to try to correct the hole and the poor blood supply. Weeks went by, and no response came.

In early summer, the Hills set off for their break with the family in Australia. They spotted a Northwest Airlines plane at the airport and smiled at each other. Northwest Airlines had covered the costs for Molly and Kaitlyn's travel to have surgery. They had also just held a raffle where the pilots and staff had raised a further $20,000 towards the foster home's new extension.

Kaitlyn loved meeting her new family and the Hills had a

chance to spend some time with their older children. When they got home to China they found that many of the babies were now able to toddle or shuffle their way over to welcome them back. It was now a year and a half since the Hills had moved into Hope Foster Home, and it looked as though the new play equipment for outside would arrive just in time for these rapidly growing children.

Joyce took three of her babies to a Tianjin hospital to see whether a visiting orthopaedic surgeon from Stanford University in the USA could help them. While she was waiting she noticed a baby crying alone in a hospital cot. The baby had been brought from a local CWI to be examined by the same surgeon, but she was running a fever and whimpering with pain. She was also evidently hungry, but there did not seem to be anyone who was looking after the sick and frightened child. Joyce was not allowed to begin interfering with a hospital patient, so she was unable to do anything but sit and look on. Eventually someone came to feed the baby, and then the surgeon arrived to examine her.

The surgeon suspected a joint infection and drew a sample of fluid from the baby's hip with a needle, but there was no sign of any pus or infection. He was due to fly back out to America the next day and could do no further investigations. The child was sent back to her CWI, but Joyce could not find out which one. She went home unable to forget the baby's face, so full of pain, and wished that she could have helped.

Not long after, Joyce heard from the Stanford surgeon again. He had not been able to forget the baby either, and had been very unhappy to leave her without making a diagnosis. He wanted to follow up the case, but had been unable to trace the baby at her CWI. Out of the blue, he emailed Joyce. Could she help him find the baby?

He was able to give Joyce the name of the baby's CWI, but the only clue he could give her about the baby was that over a year ago she had been wearing a T-shirt with the name Alice on the front. It wasn't a lot of information to locate a child in a CWI of several hundred children, but Joyce was determined to find her. She felt sure that if she saw the girl she would recognize her sad and malnourished little face.

Joyce knew the director of the CWI and went to her office to explain that a surgeon who had tried to help one of her babies had asked her to come and find out how the child was getting on.

"All I know is that the baby was wearing a T-shirt with the name Alice on it," Joyce offered.

The director nodded. "Yes," she said, "I do remember her trip to the hospital. I'll go and fetch her."

Joyce was overjoyed to recognize the child, but she was now skin and bone with a large and bloated tummy. At seventeen months she had never stood or walked because of her painful hip deformity. When Joyce held her, she could feel that one of her hips was completely out of joint. It was hard to see a child suffering and in such a condition. The director was more than happy for Joyce to take the little girl (later named Bethany) back to the foster home to see if anything could be done.

When Joyce brought Bethany back home to Beijing, she assigned the baby her own nanny, since she was going to need a lot of care. Bethany had spent much of her life in pain and was a frightened and wary little girl. She would cling onto her nanny if she saw someone new, but gradually she began to get to know the other babies and nannies and to relax and play. It was a great joy to see Bethany begin to eat well and look more healthy.

If the estimate of Bethany's age was correct, according to when she was abandoned, then she was a year and a half old.

But she weighed just 8 kilos, the weight of a child half her age. Joyce had her pelvis X-rayed and immediately sent the results to a surgeon in Singapore, who confirmed that Bethany did indeed have a dislocated hip, but he could not understand why, as she did not seem to have any other orthopaedic problems. He agreed to do a surgical investigation. As soon as the paperwork could be arranged, a volunteer flew out with Bethany to the hospital in Singapore.

Bethany's surgery revealed an unusual condition: the baby had a large mass of scarring on the muscle connecting the hip to the spine. As the scarring increased, it was gradually contracting the muscle and pulling the hipbone out of the hip socket, and the muscle was too wasted by infection and poor nutrition to keep the hip in place. Bethany had been living with a great deal of pain.

The surgeon removed the scar tissue to release the muscle, reset the hip back into its socket and put the baby in a lower-spine plaster cast to help the hip settle. It would need a long recovery time with physiotherapy to build up the muscle, but Joyce was thrilled to hear that eventually Bethany would be able to learn to walk.

At three years old, Bethany took her first steps. And several years later, Joyce and Robin received a photograph of Bethany from her adoptive mother, a doctor in the USA. Bethany was on ice-skates.

But back in November 2001, while they were beginning to find help for Bethany, there was still no good news about Katherine's heart repair, and things were beginning to seem hopeless. The baby was growing weaker each day and they could find no surgeon able to help. But Rob and Joyce were not willing to accept that they would just have to sit back and watch Katherine die. She was now fourteen months old and, although tired and breathless from her complex heart problems, she was a responsive and sweet little girl. They both agreed that they should go on looking for help: Katherine was worth all that they had to make her well.

Then a reply came back from a cardiologist in Australia. Although the surgery would be difficult, he was willing to try. Joyce was moved to see how many caring people wanted to help towards Katherine's surgery costs. When Joyce set off to Perth with the blue-lipped toddler, all the necessary funds for Katherine's surgery had come in.

Joyce took Katherine to the Perth hospital and waited and prayed while the little girl underwent a series of tests. A dye was sent through the baby's arteries, giving an exact map of her blood flow, and then Joyce was called in to see the results. The surgeon seemed very subdued and asked Joyce to sit down. She listened while he outlined how the main artery supplying the baby's lungs was now completely closed. A network of tiny arteries had grown up from the main artery in an attempt to supply some blood to the lungs, but this was inadequate to supply enough blood and oxygen to her system.

It was clear that a complete repair was out of the question. The baby's only hope would be a heart–lung transplant, but the risks for Katherine were too high, the costs too great.

Joyce took Katherine back home on the plane, deeply saddened and disappointed by the outcome. The doctors at the hospital had been quite frank. Katherine could live till her teens, but not beyond that. She was a normal, bright little girl, but would have a very short life. The end for her would be painless but sudden. And sadly, this news would also limit her chances of being adopted, as it would take a very special couple or person to want to be her parents for such a short time.

Rob and Joyce were committed to making the rest of Katherine's life peaceful and happy. They took some comfort from knowing that they had done all they could to help her, and that for the rest of her life she would be loved and wanted. Many people had given so much to help Katherine. Rob and Joyce wrote to all her supporters to tell them the news and ask their permission to donate her funds to the next child who would need surgical treatment.

Katherine was simply happy to be home again in familiar surroundings. In spite of her health difficulties, she continued to do well.

It was cold and snowy that Christmas of 2001. A lot of people brought Christmas gifts for the children. The Beijing International School students (BISS) turned up with their families, and together with the Todd family, they filled up the foster home's foyer with bags and bags of baby products. The Hills watched in amazement as the bags kept on coming in.

On 16 January at 6:15 a.m., Katherine died. She had not wanted to play much for several days and had almost stopped eating. On that last morning, her nanny came to fetch Joyce and said that the little girl was not breathing very well. Joyce went to her bed and cradled Katherine in her arms. As she held her, Katherine took her last breath and her heart stopped beating.

Katherine had come to the foster home on Children's Day, seven months earlier. In China, Children's Day is celebrated on 1 June. The children are given a day off school as a thank you for being custodians of the nation's future. Joyce and Robin had been determined to do everything they could to save her, and had fought and prayed. But it was not to be.

But as the Hills, the nannies and the volunteers wept for her loss, it was as if, over the past few months, the truth about

Katherine had been revealed. She had been a small, unimportant little girl that someone had discarded on the streets of Tianjin, unknown and unloved. But for the people in the Hope Foster Home, the loss of Katherine meant that the world was now missing a child who could not be replaced, who was loved and just as important as any other person in the world. This was the real Katherine, loved by all in the Home, and by the many people worldwide who had followed her progress and supported her. At the time of her death the Hills received messages of condolence from people as far away as Vietnam, Korea, the UK, the USA, Hong Kong, Australia and New Zealand.

Katherine was a very special child who touched hearts all over the world. As her two nannies and Joyce wept together, they knew that during the last few months of her life Katherine had been treasured and had died in the arms of those who loved her.

Robin and Joyce also grieved for the two wonderful families who had wanted to adopt Katherine, despite knowing her inoperable condition.

When a loved child dies, nothing can replace that child, and it is hard to wake up each day and realize that they are gone. Not all the babies that Joyce and Robin fought to care for and save would get better. Joyce began to see how difficult it would be to live through this again and again, and yet she knew that she was willing to continue to care for and love these children, even if it was for a very short time – because that was what they deserved.

But now, they needed time to mourn Katherine.

The next few months were difficult and challenging. Many new babies arrived, and Joyce had to deal with an outbreak of pneumonia that affected eight of the babies. And in the midst of all this, some of the nannies coming in for the night shift found a small bundle of blankets deposited in front of the gate. They bent down to look in the darkness and the bundle began to cry. They panicked, ran inside and woke up Joyce. She came out and picked up the bundle. She undid the blankets and saw a little boy, very newborn and with his umbilical cord still attached. He seemed perfectly healthy and it was very late, so they washed and fed him and let him sleep.

First thing in the morning they took the child down to the police station to report the abandonment, as was legally required. The police agreed to let them take care of the child while they investigated matters.

By chance, the parents were found in the village that day, the mother still being in hospital. It was unclear whether the mother was aware that her baby was still alive. Baby Jack had been "blue" at birth and his father was afraid that the child might be mentally handicapped. There were many cultural issues involved and the Hills fully understood and sympathized with them, but Jack's welfare was the first priority, so after long negotiations with the father, they reached a compromise with the parents: the parents would take the baby home and look after him and Joyce would visit them to see how Jack was progressing. Then, if after several months they still felt that they did not want baby Jack, the Hills promised that they would take him in, no matter what condition he was in.

But when they visited Jack's family a few weeks later, it was clear that his mother had bonded closely with him. Jack was healthy and had put on weight. He was now a well-loved baby.

* * *

Now with fifteen babies, the Hope Foster Home was getting through a lot of water, but the supply was beginning to have a strange, brackish taste and the well it came from was showing signs of running dry. Constantly having to sterilize the unreliable water supply was adding a lot of work and worry, but Rob managed to arrange for the home to connect to a deeper well some distance away. He joked that they would be toasting the new building expansion, not with champagne, but with glasses of clean water straight from the tap.

In February, several babies left to be adopted, including Amelia, who went to her new family in China. Looking at all the photos of babies on the board in her office, Joyce saw that since they had moved in some two and a half years ago, twenty-three children had been a part of the Home; and of those babies, five had received surgery, five more were awaiting surgery and five had been adopted by their own families.

The garden outside was looking much greener and the children were delighted to be able to go out and explore the slide and a new playhouse. The baby animal petting farm was almost ready – a great source of amusement to the groundsman and the local builders, as most villagers kept chickens and goats for more practical reasons.

When Joyce sat down to do the monthly newsletter, she wrote, "God's hand in providing for us since we began has been nothing short of miraculous. We have lacked nothing. God provided so abundantly for our needs that, when people asked us lately what we needed, we often had to say, in all honesty, that we lacked nothing."

8

Leaving the new home

Truly, truly, I say to you, unless a grain of wheat falls into the earth and dies, it remains alone; but if it dies, it bears much fruit.

JOHN 12:24 (ESV)

By June 2002, some irreconcilable differences had arisen between Hope Foster Home and some of the other overseas personnel involved in the main community project that owned the site. Sadly, it was decided that Joyce and Robin should move out of their house and hand over the foster home to the care of the organization that had provided the land – and leave all the babies and nannies behind.

All of the children knew and loved the Hills as foster parents and five of the children, including Bethany, were in the process of undergoing surgery arranged by Joyce.

But the nannies that Joyce had trained were now all closely bonded with the babies. They were all local women, living in the small villages around the home. It would not be possible to replace all the nannies at short notice in a new area, and even if it were, they had no premises to move the babies or nannies into. For the sake of peace in the home, for the sake of the children and the nannies and the other people working in the same field, the Hills decided that they should accept the situation and move out.

Kaitlyn was their own adopted child, and Daniel's mother, who had asked Joyce to care for him again, insisted that he go with the Hills. But they would no longer be able to care for the children that they had brought from various institutions. To Joyce and Robin, the bereavement of having to leave a houseful of children, who they had looked after for two or three years as if they were their own family, was like experiencing a sudden death several times over.

They were asked to move out within two weeks.

Ryan, who had been so supportive and cheerful about starting up the foster home, and who always played with the toddlers when he came home from school, now felt hurt and angry. He was also good friends with other teenagers and families in the project and loved the village and the neighbourhood.

Ryan had just helped Rob to build a climbing wall on one side of their house and had worked hard erecting the scaffolding and then sculpting the footholds. As they were packing up to leave, he and Rob sat on the floor of the hall in their house with their backs against the wall.

"But I've only had two climbs on that wall," Ryan said.

Rob nodded. He had never seen a kid so angry before, and he wanted to help Ryan in some way. But the truth was, he was struggling himself.

"And what about my room, Dad? What about my door?"

Ryan's room was full of the usual teenage decorations and posters, but the *pièce de résistance* was his door. It was covered in his mascots and posters and a whole collection of memorabilia.

Robin stood up.

"D'you know what?" he said. "You can take your door with you."

"Can I?"

"Yep, I'll help you take it off its hinges," said Rob.

So he and Ryan took the door off its hinges and put it in the car.

The nannies and staff were close friends with the Hills. They too felt hurt and angry but Joyce asked them to stay on and look after the babies and keep their jobs. Linda, who had always looked after Katie, could not stop weeping, and Xiao Jun knelt on the floor with her head in Joyce's lap and cried until Joyce's clothes were soaked through with tears. Their driver Xiao Li was a tall young man who was always cheerful and cavalier about life, but now he too stood crying. He offered to go and find some local "heavies" to sort out the situation, which the Hills explained was not what they wanted or needed right then.

The Hills were now without their home or ministry and were simply unable to contemplate starting over. They were not even sure if they wanted to stay in China – perhaps it was time to go home. It was not an experience that Joyce had expected to go through at the age of fifty. She said about that time:

"I had had enough. Everything had been taken away from me: my children, my home, my reputation, my money. I had nothing left. I was praying about it but I was really angry with God. I thought, 'Why, when I obeyed every word that you said?' But then, I felt God say, 'It was easy to obey me when you had everything. Will you still obey me now, when you have nothing?' It was a turning point for me: what does obedience mean? And I could see that it meant obedience – no matter what. But I didn't know how to go on: I had had enough."

But then people in their church began to gather round them. Although they did not know him very well, a church member named Toby Littlewood was one of the first people to come up to

Robin and Joyce and say, "You can't leave China, not after all the work that you have done."

"But we have nothing to stay for," Joyce explained. "All the avenues have been blocked."

When Toby heard that they had to move out of their house and had nowhere else to go, he quickly telephoned his wife, Jing. The Littlewoods were in the process of selling a house, and Jing was about to set off for the lawyer's office to sign the sales agreement, and had been on the phone talking to the estate agent to finalize the details. But the moment she finished her call, the phone rang again.

"Has the sale gone through yet?" Toby asked.

"Not quite," she told him.

"Good, because Robin and Joyce might want to move in. Rob's going to call you."

As Jing put the phone down, the other line rang. It was Robin.

"Is the house still available?" he asked.

"Yes, if you want it," Jing replied. She heard his voice catch as he softly said, "Thank you."

"The funny thing is," Jing later told Joyce, "that after we bought it, we talked about this house being used for Christian ministry in some way. I had a word that it would be used to help orphans, and until that day, I didn't see how that could be."

So Toby and Jing took the Hill family to see a smart three-storey house in a leafy, gated estate called Capital Paradise, near to Beijing. There would be plenty of facilities at hand, and Ryan's school was just a walk around the corner.

Shortly afterwards, another friend at church called Fred Hsu rang Joyce and said, "I need you to meet with me and sign some papers."

"But what papers?" said Joyce.

"Just meet up with me and I've got something for you to sign."

Mystified, Robin and Joyce met Fred and, to their amazement, found that he had been over to Hong Kong and purchased a company. He wanted to give it to the Hills so that they could have a legal presence to function in China.

Again, Fred was more of an acquaintance than a close friend at the time, and they were amazed that he should be moved to do so much to help them start to care for children with needs again.

But worried by such generosity, Joyce asked Fred how much the company had cost him. "Listen," he said, "what you have done for the children is priceless compared to what I am giving you."

It was incredibly generous, yet Joyce still felt reservations. They had lost so much. Would they lose more if she signed these documents? Then she heard a soft voice, almost a chuckle in her heart that brought a smile to her face: "You have lost everything. You have nothing more to lose."

So they became owners of a company that would allow them to officially open a foster home and start over again.

In July, Joyce and Robin went back to Australia for a break with the family. They had a wonderfully restful time, and their friends and family helped tremendously in the healing process. They were very tempted to stay in Australia, but both felt that the work they had to do in China was not yet finished. On the way home they stopped in Singapore to pick up Bethany The Hills would then accompany her back to the original foster home. It was going to be hard to say goodbye to Bethany once more, but she would be returning to the care of the nannies she had bonded with so closely and the home that she was familiar with. They were able to meet the team of surgeons, who were delighted to find Bethany looking wonderfully well and making good progress towards walking.

As they landed at Beijing Airport with Katie and Bethany, Rob and Joyce could not help wondering what lay ahead, and they got off the plane with very mixed feelings. But as they came through Customs they saw three Chinese people – Linda, Xiao Jun and Xiao Li – waiting to meet them. Linda rushed over to hug and kiss Katie, whom she had helped care for so well since she was a baby. Xiao Li, the driver – who knew all the thugs in the neighbourhood and who had been so keen to bring round a group of heavies to sort the situation out – was now bursting to tell them that he had decided to become a Christian while they were away. As Robin stared at him, he thought, "How did you manage that, God, in all this mess?"

They announced to Robin and Joyce that they had all resigned their posts, and were ready to work for them as soon as they started the new home.

Robin and Joyce were both thinking the same thing. At a meeting at the old home, a friend had prayed for them and seen a picture in which three Chinese people would carry them along through this time of trouble. The friend saw the Hills being given a lift on bicycles by the three people. The friend told them, "I think these three Chinese people are going to be very important to you in the future." The Hills had thought it referred to the people in the meeting at the time, but over the next few years they were to find that the three people who had met them that day at the airport would have key roles in developing the work with needy children, with Xiao Li being a dependable driver in tricky situations, Xiao Jun helping to manage and run the home in Beijing, and Linda growing in confidence and skills to run the children's units that they would one day open in Henan.

Without Robin and Joyce even needing to ask one person to donate, money began to arrive so that they could start to build Hope Foster Home 2. The kindness and support of friends was overwhelming.

But once they were back home in their new house, the Hill family agreed that what they now needed was time to be together quietly and come to terms with what had happened. That time, however, was to prove very short indeed. "We were licking our wounds," said Joyce, "and then people started to bring us children."

Joyce got a call from Marsha, a Beijing resident who did a lot of work with Children's Welfare Institutes in the area, and particularly with the Philip Hayden Foundation, which fostered many needy children. Marsha had a real heart for orphans and was always being asked by various organizations to help with practicalities such as paperwork and placing children in suitable foster care. She kept the phone numbers of any people she thought might be useful, and was able to put the right people in touch with one another. She now had a little girl with a heart condition in a CWI who needed a foster family. As a doctor, Joyce would be ideal as a foster mum. Would Joyce consider taking her on?

So as Christmas 2002 approached, and even though they were not quite ready, Joyce and Robin decided that it was time to take in the first new baby of Hope Foster Home 2. Baby Charmaine arrived and was soon taking her baths in the sink, as she was still very small for her age. She was eighteen months old but had been born with a severe heart condition and was malnourished. They took her to Beijing United Family Hospital to investigate her condition and to begin treatment to make her stronger.

Just before Christmas, Charmaine received a present from

a little girl aged seven who lived in the USA. Lindsey had read about Charmaine in Joyce's newsletters and saved up to buy a special Christmas gift for the baby, probably the first gift that Charmaine had ever received in her life. Joyce was also touched to receive a donation from Rebecca Sweeny, who was twelve and had raised funds by herself.

If the Hills were to start to take in children once more, they needed to find a piece of land, or a building they could convert. Xiao Li, the driver, kept his ear to the ground and came back with three possibilities. The first was a huge institution that was too impersonal to make a home for children. The next was a disused factory that was very run down and dirty, with a sinister red cat statue waving one mechanical arm forlornly. The third was the unfinished shell of a new school, now for sale.

They drove out on the long, straight roads of the Chinese farmland, lined with rows of newly planted willow trees, and came to a two-storey building in the middle of fields of maize and sweet potatoes. It needed floors, heating, windows and fitting out, but once finished, it would have enough space for them to start with twenty-four babies, or perhaps as many as thirty-six.

They had a small, designated building fund, but they were really going to need three times as much again. Robin and Joyce met with the newly convened Board of Directors for "New Hope Foster Home", which now included Toby Littlewood and Fred Hsu, to discuss the plans to purchase the building.

Robin explained that there was a serious problem. It was not possible to own the land outright: they could never be secure tenants and there would always be a risk that they could lose the building and all the refurbishment costs – and this would apply to most sites.

"Well," said Fred, "if we wait till all the i's are dotted and all the t's are crossed, Jesus will have come back and you won't need a foster home."

So the Board agreed that the funds should be released to start to convert the building shell into a home, and once again Rob set off on the trail of planning, costing, and meetings with builders, plumbers and electricians – approaching the large and rather daunting project with cheerful relish. He found that all his skills in managing projects at Sandvik served him well, as did his energy and his gift for seeing a new way into a problem.

As Robin and Joyce drew up the floor plans to convert the school to babies' bedrooms, playrooms, an isolation ward and living space, they began to realize that they would end up with spacious and flexible accommodation, and much more scope to expand the numbers of babies that they took in.

"It was an interesting thing," Rob says. "One of the things that God wrote into my heart at that time was, unless the seed falls into the ground and dies, it can't bear fruit. At the time, we were watching everything fall apart around us. All of the dreams, and the vision that we thought was really from God – we were watching that dying. And then we had that word. Now we're able to look back, some five or ten years later, and see that yes, God did plant a small seed that carried on, and it doubled and quadrupled and really did help kids. At the time, with human eyes, it looked like a failure, and yet it certainly wasn't. That home we left kept going, and we went on to a project that kept expanding."

Joyce had another couple of calls from Marsha asking for help, and so two more babies with heart problems joined the family. Both babies were very skinny and underweight and in need of building up. Linda and Xiao Jun came in each day to help with childcare. It was a tight fit but the house was comfortable and modern and it was wonderful to have the pool at the clubhouse.

A few steps down a leafy avenue was a play park for the children. Joyce looked for double strollers for the nannies, but found they were not on sale in China. She put out a special request in the newsletter for people who were returning to Beijing after the holidays to bring a stroller back with them if at all possible, and the nannies were soon proudly pushing them out to the park.

Joyce and Robin were thankful that they had been able to complete the surgical arrangements for their remaining children in the first foster home, and were glad to hear that Bethany was continuing to make very good progress. It was also a great joy to have the chance to meet the new parents of Claire. Two years earlier, Rob had asked Joyce to take her as an extra child as they left a CWI and had said, "Look, if we don't take this one she will die." Her new parents, a young Canadian couple, came round to share a meal with Robin and Joyce and hear about Claire's early days in the home. Several other families came to say goodbye as the children left to go home with their forever families, including a bonny little Sophie, hard to recognize as the same baby who had once been so very undernourished and hard to feed. In the years to come Joyce was delighted to receive many new photos of the children as they grew up into thriving young men and poised and beautiful young women, sent by their proud and loving families.

9

New Hope

When we lose one blessing, another is often, most unexpectedly, given in its place.

C. S. Lewis

In January 2003, Joyce was sent a two-year-old boy called Evan who was so weak that he could not lift his head and needed a lot of care to build him up after heart surgery. Three weeks later, on Chinese New Year's Day, Evan took his first steps. The streets across Beijing were banging and exploding with firecrackers as all families were at home together celebrating, but no one was celebrating more than the Hills as they all applauded Evan's first shaky steps around the cramped sitting room. Charmaine was also walking, and the Hill family, the four babies and their nannies could still just about fit into a house intended for a family of four people, but it was good to see how much progress was being made on the New Hope Foster Home out at Shunyi.

If you want a job doing, then Rob is the man to do it, and work inside the building continued at a pace. The converted school shell was starting to look like a habitable building and there was just the decorating and the final fitting left to do.

But outside, standing in the middle of a field of grey earth, the building looked like it had been dropped on the surface of the moon. As Joyce and Robin watched the March winds swirling the dust around them in grey clouds, Rob said, "We really need some trees along the west perimeter to provide some shelter." But Joyce reminded him that at that early stage funds were limited and they had a lot of things to put in that were more urgent. The garden was going to have to be a long-term project.

But as they looked at the grim expanse of dirt, they could both see that the dust was going to be a problem. One of the features of the land around Beijing is the fine, grey dust that insidiously settles on all surfaces. If left unchecked it can build up and make everything look grey and grubby. New arrivals to the city soon learn why everyone takes off their outdoor shoes before going inside.

As the babies grew and developed in the new home, it was going to be important for them to have the chance to play on the floor, to learn to sit up and roll over and so develop their muscle tone and coordination. With the garden unplanted, it was also going to be a constant struggle to keep the floor clean enough for the babies to lie on and play, or go barefoot in warm weather. Amber and Joyce had spent a lot of time convincing the nannies that it was a good thing to let the babies walk around in bare feet to improve their balance, but children running round in bare feet on a dusty Beijing floor was going to mean very black little feet.

Robin and Joyce drove back to the house on the Capital Paradise estate, trying to think of an answer, but failing to come up with any solutions.

Five minutes after they walked into the house, the phone rang and Rob answered it.

"You don't know me," said a voice, "but I work with Shell. We heard that you are starting a home for orphans. Would you like some trees?"

Rob was speechless, not sure whether to laugh or cry, but managed to say, "Yes please." Within two weeks Shell delivered 138 trees to the site, along with gardeners to plant them out.

Rob said later, "We couldn't see how to sort that problem, then I picked up the phone and a woman offered us exactly what we needed. I was gobsmacked. Problem solved by an amazing God who knows what you need before you even ask."

If you fast-forward to a few years later, then it seems as if the gracious lines of trees have always been there. The weeping willows form a delicate green curtain around the perimeter of the garden and sway in the breeze, like a line of traditional Chinese dancers in trailing robes – and every so often, two or three magpies fly up, looking remarkably like fluttering fans. In summer the branches are full of the chirping of sparrows and a constant chorus of cicadas that sound like hundreds of tiny watches unwinding. Teams of volunteers have also turned the mud into a lovely garden, with lawns, paths and a play park for the children.

It is a very different scene from the worrying dust bowl that greeted the Hills that day. Any visit to the home now will show you babies on the floor – playing, kicking on blankets, or simply having a nap. And to keep the bamboo flooring spotless, there is always a cleaner going along the sunny corridor and through the playrooms with her trusty mop and bucket. In fact it is hard to walk through the building along the gleaming corridors without meeting a lady with a mop going over the floor once again.

As the new building and gardens came together, Robin and Joyce were both very aware of how privileged they felt to be able to stay in China and continue to care for the children. Through the internet letter, people had adopted rooms in the home, or sponsored nannies, or given washing machines, fridges, high chairs and all the various practical things needed to care for a houseful of children. It seemed as though a community of people had come together like some village of hope in the ether, united by the will to care for those children who had once been abandoned without hope.

In March, Rob received the sad news that his father had passed away, and they flew back to attend his funeral in the British Midlands. Rob's father had been a caring and active person in the community, and over 500 people came to his funeral to say goodbye.

A great deal of healing had taken place between Rob and his dad since Rob left home as an angry teenager, feeling that his dad cared more for church than for him – his dad never had time to take him to football or fishing. But over the years, as Rob trusted the Father, he began to see his dad as someone who was trying to do the best he could.

When his father was seventy, Rob took him on a fishing trip in New Zealand and was thrilled when his dad landed a fish. It was a day that seemed to symbolize how much had been restored to them as father and son.

Rob's dad had always been very proud and supportive of their work with the children in China. When he died, people gave to the Home in lieu of sending flowers. He had also left Rob a small bequest, enough to build a small home for the immediate Hill family beside the New Hope Foster Home, and also expand the main building so that they could take in a further twelve babies.

When they returned to China, Joyce and Rob were contacted by local CWIs inviting them to visit and see which children they might be able to help. They travelled out through the busy towns and quiet farmland of Hebei province to visit a small orphanage that was being run by a Roman Catholic nun. It was a very cold day, but inside the home's little white building with its tiny clock-tower, the children were bright-cheeked and warmly dressed.

Although the director there did not have a lot of resources, she was doing a marvellous job caring for the children. They were clean and well loved and the building was homely and well run. The Sister was very clear that every child in her care was "Jesus" to her, and as Robin and Joyce looked around the home that she ran so well, on limited means, they knew that they wanted to have the same spirit of care for each and every child. Joyce agreed to take three children from the home and try to find surgeons to correct the babies' problems, including baby Gene, who had a badly infected colostomy opening. The tiny baby colostomy bags needed were not obtainable and the home was having to use bags that were far too large for the opening.

Beijing and the surrounding areas became unusually quiet as everyone stayed home, as directed during the SARS epidemic. Robin and Joyce had to field a lot of enquiries checking that they were well, as the SARS outbreak was constantly on the worldwide news. In fact they had no problem with the SARS flu in the house in Capital Paradise estate. Joyce began a twice-daily regime of disinfecting all contact points in the little house, even shampoo bottles and light switches. This system is still in place today in the larger home, and contributes to the fact that even though a child has on one occasion come home from a hospital with an MRSA infection, the Hope Foster Homes have never had an outbreak of any MRSA bugs among the children.

* * *

Just before they moved out of the Capital Paradise house, Joyce got a phone call from a Chinese lawyer from Singapore called JT. He was involved with supporting community projects in China, and one of the community workers he supported had recently been asked to look after an abandoned baby by a local doctor. The child was severely handicapped, however, and they needed advice about how best to care for his special needs.

When the little boy was born, his parents left him in the hospital and disappeared. A doctor there took him to the local CWI, but they saw that he had cerebral palsy and so told her that there was nothing to be done for him. She argued with the CWI to provide the care he needed to survive, but they said, "Well, what do you want him to live for?"

The doctor somehow knew about the community worker and so contacted him. He and his wife agreed to take the child in and care for him. Baby Nico was a chubby baby and not sick, but he did not respond to sound or light. The couple asked JT if he could find a doctor to assess the baby's needs. He heard about Joyce and gave her a call.

After she had examined the baby and sent him for a full CT scan, Joyce did not have good news for them: "I'm afraid he is blind and deaf, and I'm very sorry to say that he is also developmentally delayed. There isn't much of a normal future for him."

Joyce knew that it would be a very hard burden for a family with already limited means to meet the needs of such a profoundly handicapped child. She held the small weight of the baby in her arms, and felt that it was right to offer to care for Nico at New Hope. It would be a long-term commitment and she did not have the funds needed in place, but Joyce focused on the fact that she knew this was going to be the best chance for baby Nico to find the care he needed.

JT had the same heart to see Nico have the best possible chance in life. Without hesitating, he undertook to cover all the expenses needed for Nico's care.

* * *

The neighbours in Capital Paradise must surely have been wondering how many babies it was possible to squeeze into one ordinary semi-detached house. But in the early summer of 2003 the Hills were finally able to start moving into New Hope Foster Home. On 28 July, Evan, Hayley, Charmaine, Daniel, Nico and Gene all slept in their new cots for the first time. Two night nannies sat nearby with a night lamp on, quietly chatting as they kept an eye on the sleeping children.

Robin, Joyce, Ryan and Katy moved into the small family flat on the upper storey of the building. From the back windows was a view over acres of maize and sweet potatoes where swallows and their shadows endlessly crisscrossed the fields. In the distance, white egrets and herons could be seen, flapping lazily from wide fishponds. From the front, beyond the garden, you could see the road to the village, with bicycles flickering through the rows of willow trees as people cycled to and from their work in the fields. Screens at the windows throughout the building helped keep out the very healthy-looking countryside crickets and bugs while still letting a breeze through the building, but as the summer grew hotter, it would be a question of shutting all the windows and turning on the air conditioning.

Rob and Ryan set out the old train set in one corner of the office and Hayley and Evan were constant visitors each morning, toddling up to the office after breakfast with their nannies to sit and watch the trains go round. Evan, who looked such a little live wire, liked to sit and thoughtfully watch the trains, while Hayley, with a bow in her hair and looking as if butter would not melt in her mouth, was very keen to swipe one of the trains whenever she could.

Just below the Hills' flat was the kitchen. From 5 a.m. each morning came the sound of enthusiastic chopping, as the cook started preparing meals, using plenty of fresh vegetables. Ryan and Katie were looking forward to being able to sleep in a little longer in the morning when they eventually moved into the family cottage that Rob was planning to build alongside the main home.

Sometimes it was hard to believe only a year had gone by since they had had to leave behind all that they had started, but though it was good to be in the new home, Joyce was aware that she still felt cautious about their future.

The past year had been a hard lesson in not expecting things to run in a straight line. It had thrown them onto having to trust, when they could not even begin to understand the reason for things happening. Joyce said, "Sometimes, stepping out in faith can be a very lonely place. But people around us supported and encouraged us in every possible way. We saw miracle after miracle happen during that time, and all those people were tremendously important in making that happen: the encouragement, the donations, the people who turned up to clean – and boy, did we clean! – and the people who came and planted trees and shrubs. He just gathered people round us, and we felt His love and guidance and strength. In the end we felt even closer to each other and to God."

Four weeks after they moved into the new home, Robin and Joyce took in the first new babies with unmet medical needs. They all settled in well, but a few nights later, Nico and Charmaine had severe seizures and it was a mad rush in the middle of the night to get them to the hospital in time. The doctors fought hard to keep the children alive. The nannies wept to see the children in pain. But by the morning the children were sleeping calmly and there was an enormous feeling of relief that both the children had pulled through.

One of the first new babies to arrive at New Hope was little Zachary, who arrived on the night train as an emergency case. There were some complications for Zachary in hospital. The opening in his tummy became infected and when he came home to New Hope, Joyce cried to see his wound so badly infected. He was emaciated, poorly, and his little head had been shaved for the drip. But Joyce managed to clear up the stomach wound and with careful nursing and diligent feeding Zachary began to fill out into a thoughtful and handsome little boy who made everyone feel glad to have the chance to know him.

Zachary had been abandoned on the street. He had been seen as untreatable by his carers and expected to die. But three years later, he was to begin a new life in the USA, where his adoptive mother ran a horse ranch. And when she entered him in the local contest to find the most beautiful baby in the town, he was awarded first place.

10

Life in the new home

Whatever you did for one of the least of these brothers of mine, you did for me.

MATTHEW 25:40

One hundred and fifty guests braved the foggy weather for the official opening of the New Hope Foster Home on 1 November 2003. Students from the International School helped to pass round mugs of hot tea to the warmly dressed people seated on rows of folding chairs in the misty garden, while other students provided a small orchestra to entertain the guests. For the Hills, it was a wonderful blessing to see how many people shared the same vision to help the children and bless others with their "servant hearts".

Robin and Joyce stood under the awning of the front porch with Party Secretary Mr Wang, Town Mayor Mr Zhou, and the wives of the British and German ambassadors, to declare the New Hope Foster Home officially open. Joyce, in her splendid red Chinese jacket and black trousers, found that she had managed to coordinate perfectly with the outfits of the other ladies as well as the grey foggy weather.

The children and nannies watched proceedings from the windows, as it was too cold to have the babies outside. Joyce felt very proud of all her nannies. They were caring for children with conditions that could have been alarming in a culture where traditionally few handicapped children are seen, but they truly loved the children, doing all the small tasks that take place between a mother and child. The nannies were also having to get used to the extra procedures needed for medically fragile babies, such as carrying out dilation treatments for the children who had undergone anal repairs, using the special feeding bottles for babies with cleft palates, or watching carefully for fevers or other symptoms in children recovering from heart operations. And all the while the nannies provided a cheerful, family atmosphere.

Most of the children had come to New Hope from a situation with a ratio of one carer to twenty or thirty children. In the New Hope Foster Home the same two children were able to always have the same two nannies; one nanny for the morning and one for the afternoon. At night, one nanny would look after four sleeping children but always stayed awake all the night in case the children became sick or needed help. In this way the babies were able to make good relationships as a model for later life, and Joyce often heard back from adoptive parents that the children had been able to bond quickly and well with their new parents.

Nico was not doing very well again. He continued to have distressing seizures. In November he developed severe pneumonia and died. His nannies and Joyce wept when they realized that he had gone. It was the first time that a baby had died in the new home, and everyone felt the loss of this small boy.

Baby Nico had been left unwanted in a hospital ward, and he had had a short and very limited life, with cerebral palsy and no hearing and vision. But during that short life, Nico had been truly loved and wanted, and made as happy and comfortable as possible.

His ashes were buried in the garden and over them a tree was planted that could always be seen from the window of Joyce and Robin's home.

As autumn came round again and the cold winds blew in, Joyce found that she was experiencing a very specific and debilitating kind of headache. As soon as she got up in the morning, a pain would hit her like a blow to the head and remain so long as she stood upright. It was a return of an old problem, where suspension fluid from the brain was leaking out through a minute hole, leaving her brain fluid depleted and the brain pressing down on her spinal cord.

Joyce flew to Hong Kong for investigative treatment. The surgeons tried to locate a possible leak in the spine so that it could be patched with a blood clot, but were unable to find it. They told Joyce that there was nothing more they could do, since it was most likely to be a leak located in the brain membrane. However, Joyce was relieved to find that when she got home, she did get respite from the headaches for many months.

Rob had kept everything shipshape and running smoothly while she was away, and as they approached the end of their first year, New Hope was filled to capacity. As Joyce looked around the sleeping children that evening in their brightly painted rooms, beneath quilt covers she had sewn for them, she felt a great sense of peace.

Joyce got straight down to trying to find help for the several babies in need of heart surgery. Hayley's case was the most urgent. As Christmas approached Joyce got the go-ahead from a surgeon in New York and so she requested the baby's passport from her CWI. The dates for Hayley's travel and surgery were set, and they prayed that everything would go smoothly.

All through Christmas they were kept very busy caring for

six babies with delicate hearts, and Joyce often felt as if she was running a cardiac hospital. The supplies of specialist heart medication needed to keep the babies' hearts in good condition were beginning to run very low. Joyce posted a request for help through the newsletter, and was overwhelmed to find that enough medication to last a couple of years was rapidly sent back.

Just after Christmas, the director from Hayley's CWI rang with bad news. Her passport had been stolen from his office. He was very upset and promised to apply for a new one immediately, but this would still mean a significant delay. Joyce was not sure if Hayley' heart was strong enough to survive the wait.

But in March, Hayley's passport suddenly arrived, and a volunteer and Hayley flew straight out to New York. Joyce was relieved to hear that the complex operation was fully successful. Hayley would soon be back home to wait for her adoption process to be completed, and her new mum and dad could come and take home a delightful and very healthy little girl.

Joyce set up her office with a small table where she could carry out minor surgical repairs. Toby was a sleepy teddy bear of a baby who arrived in February 2004 with fused fingers and clubbed feet. It was two weeks later than Joyce would have liked to begin the procedure, but she began to cast Toby's feet to mould them into a good shape for walking. She gave the baby a safe dose of anaesthetic and then snipped the tendon at the base of each ankle. She then gently pushed the foot into its new position and pulled on stockinet castings to set the foot into the new shape. His nanny held the baby's hands throughout, crying when the baby whimpered.

Sleepy from the anaesthetic shot, Toby went down in his cot, sucking on his comforter. He would now be able to grow up to walk without problems and pain. But looking down at the baby,

Rob said, "Maybe if his mother had known that we could do this operation for free, she might not have abandoned him."

It was a hard question to consider. Rob and Joyce knew that they did not have any solutions, only questions and thoughts and lots of love for the baby Tobys of China.

After eight months in the new home, Robin and Joyce found they were fast running out of space. Joyce had squeezed fifteen babies into rooms that were designed for just twelve. Using Rob's father's bequest, they began to build the small home for the immediate family and so free up more rooms in the main building, and also add on an extension that would allow them to take in twice as many babies. So in March 2004 the builders arrived and Joyce got out her quilting materials to begin some new sets of cot covers.

11

The twins

Do not go where the path may lead, go instead where there is no path and leave a trail.

RALPH WALDO EMERSON

In October 2003 two baby girls were abandoned in front of a CWI in Henan. The babies were only three days old and had tiny, heart-shaped faces, each a mirror image of the other. They also had identical gaps in their top lips and a gap in the soft tissue at the roof of the mouth. A cleft palate means that a baby is unable to grip and suck for herself from a normal hard bottle, and both girls were underfed and in danger of becoming seriously malnourished.

At the time, it was not possible in China to buy the kind of specialist feeding bottle needed for such children, where the soft plastic body of the bottle and the wide teat allow milk to be gently squeezed into the mouth of a baby. The only way for the CWI nannies to feed cleft-palate babies was to painstakingly spoon-feed them bit by bit. For the twins, just getting them to eat enough would take an enormous amount of time, and this was in a situation where a nanny would probably already have thirty other children to feed and care for.

But at the girls' CWI there was a volunteer called Linda Shum. She had brought a supply of special Mead Johnson feeding bottles with her from Australia, so she and the nannies were able to begin feeding formula to the premature twins straight away. This meant that Reagan and Sydney did not suffer from the malnutrition problems that are so common in cleft-palate newborns – common because the babies simply cannot feed.

Linda was due to return home to Australia, but knew that the girls were still going to need considerable care if they were to survive. The staff had mentioned how a baby called Russell with a hip deformity had gone to a foster home near Beijing, so Linda contacted Joyce. With the CWI's blessing, she drove overnight to get the twins to Beijing, hoping that the girls would be strong enough to survive the trip. It was an experience she would never forget, stopping often to feed them a little, and trying to follow the map through the dark and silent countryside where all road signs are in Chinese.

It was a great relief to get to Shun Yi and deliver the girls safely to Joyce. They were so tiny and premature that each baby weighed just two kilos. Rob could actually fit one of them into the palm of his hand.

Joyce had supplies of the specially designed feeding bottles ready. The girls were given a good feed, bathed and settled in the nursery alongside each other, in soft new baby clothes. Their new nannies were thrilled to have the chance to look after such dear little twin moppets.

Linda told Robin and Joyce that a note had been left with the babies, written on a piece of crumpled brown paper bag – probably the only paper that the parents had at the time. It said:

Dear caring people,
    We are poor and unable to provide for our twins.
Please keep them. They were born 2003, September 12th.

The carefully worded note and the unusual choice of language showed that the parents cared very much indeed about what happened to their girls. As Joyce and Robin looked at the babies, now sleeping in their cots, they reflected on how sad it was that the parents – probably poor workers or farmers – had felt they had to abandon their children, as the only means they could think of to get them the help they needed to live.

Sydney and Reagan's nannies learned how to feed them with painstaking care, as the babies' difficulty in swallowing meant that milk could easily get down their ear tubes, or into their lungs and cause a dangerous reaction. But the girls were real little fighters, and fed with gusto. They were soon putting on weight and starting to grow and fill out.

Joyce was trying to arrange surgery for the girls' cleft-lip repairs, and then for the subsequent operations needed to close the gap in the roof of their mouths. They were beautiful babies, and already had the hearts of everyone who looked after them. Joyce could not wait to see them after the cleft repair was done, when the whole world would be able to see just how beautiful the girls truly were. When they were about six months old, Joyce found out that an organization in America called Love Without Boundaries was bringing a team of US surgeons out to Shantou in China to do cleft-lip repairs. She contacted Amy Eldridge, the LWB director, and asked if the twins could be included on the surgeons' list. Amy replied to say that if Joyce could get them to Shantou in time, then they were happy to do the repairs for both girls.

Shantou is 2,000 kilometres south of Beijing, a long and tiring journey. Joyce and their nanny Sonia loaded the girls into the van along with a large bag of supplies and set off with Xiao Li driving. By the time they arrived, a couple of days later, the surgeries had already started.

Dr John Padilla and Dr Lisa David had flown out from Beverly Hills, California. Dr Lisa, an attractive and successful surgeon, had had a cleft lip and palate as a baby, and now worked at the cranial facial centre at Wake Forest University, North Carolina. Dr John was a renowned plastic surgeon from Beverly Hills who specialized in cosmetic surgery for the stars of Hollywood. Both were committed to do all they could to see that children did not have to live with the needless difficulties that come from unrepaired cleft lips.

But when John and Lisa began to assess the babies waiting for surgery, they were forced to turn away several children because they were suffering from poor feeding. Time after time, they had to say no: the babies simply did not have enough skin and fat in their lips to make surgery possible. Some of the babies brought in were so weak that the surgeons did not think they would be able to survive the anaesthesia.

So when Joyce and the nannies brought the twins in to be assessed, she was surprised to see Dr John begin to cry. It was the first time that Lisa and John had seen cleft-palate babies who were a normal weight, and even fat! Sydney and Reagan had received proper nutrition from the day that they were found, thanks to Linda, and then had continued to be properly fed at New Hope. Dr John was very excited and told Joyce that he was going to really enjoy doing an excellent repair on the girls' lips. (Dr John was later to die tragically in a plane crash, but in the week before he died, he spoke on the phone with the girls' adoptive father, and told him that seeing the girls had been a tremendous uplift for him because here were children who had been well fed and so were able to receive the best surgical repairs.)

The girls' surgery went very well. They sat side by side in their hospital cot, each with a bandage in the same place, still woozy from the anaesthetic, but cheerful and recovering very fast. Once the bandages were removed, it was wonderful to see them with their healthy upper lips and gummy new smiles.

The repairs would not only mean that they could feed, talk and socialize without problems, but also meant that the babies could be placed on the lists of the Chinese Centre for Adoption Affairs, and perhaps go forward one day to find their own forever family.

Around about the time the twins were born, a couple in Florida called Grace and Don White decided to travel to China. Don was a gifted and wise speaker, delivering successful business seminars across several countries. For twenty years Don had also put his considerable energy into a charity called the Million Dollar Round Table Foundation. In the summer of 2003 he got an email from this Foundation asking for volunteers to help construct a new playground at a foster home in China. He showed the email to Grace. Although they had travelled all over the world, they had never been to China, so, on the spur of the moment, Don emailed back and said they were in.

In January 2004, when the twins were about four months old, Grace and Don flew out to China to help build a new playground in the grounds of the Philip Hayden foster homes, just south of Beijing.

The Whites found that they enjoyed the company of Tim and Pam Baker a great deal. There was also plenty of time to get to know them as, with such an enthusiastic team on the job, the playground was finished three days ahead of schedule. Don and Grace had always wanted children. They had tried for a family and looked into adoption, but it had never worked out for them. In their late forties, they had settled into accepting that life was still fulfilling for them as a couple. But the Bakers encouraged them to think again. They said, "You know, you guys should seriously consider adopting a couple of kids from China."

Grace and Don had no idea how you went about doing such a thing. The Bakers gave them the details of A Helping Hand, an international adoption agency in America that helps families to adopt from countries such as China. As soon as they got back to Florida the Whites contacted the agency, and things started to happen.

Suddenly, the possibility of adopting was very much a reality. Grace wanted to take a pause, think things through carefully, and make sure that they were doing the right thing, but she quickly came to the conclusion that this was something she felt she could do. Although there had been many disappointments in the past, Grace now became very excited about the thought of being a mum. They decided to put themselves on the list to adopt.

Since they were in their mid forties, Don and Grace decided it would be a good thing to adopt two children at the same time. But when they spoke to the adoption agencies the answer was always the same: China did not permit double adoptions, unless twins came up! And twins, they were told, almost never came up.

A Helping Hand and the American Immigration Department both told them that if they requested twins, it was so unlikely to happen that it was hardly worth applying, since once their dossier came to the top of the queue, then they would get passed over and risk not being matched with a child.

"The problem is, Mr White," explained the girl at A Helping Hand, "we've just never had twins here."

"Well, it sounds like you're due," Don said.

The girl laughed. "Look, don't get your hopes up," she said.

"By the way, how much is all this going to cost?" Don asked.

"Well currently, it's about $14,000 to adopt from China, when you count in all the expenses and the fees."

"OK. Well, so do we get a discount for twins?" Don joked.

The girl did not see this as a funny comment.

"Everything just doubles," she told him, "so you'll be looking at fees of around $28,000."

Don assured her that that was no problem, and he and Grace went home to fill in their application forms.

Applying for only one child seemed like good and very sound advice. However, something happened just three days later that made Don and Grace feel convinced that they should apply for twins.

Don got a phone call out of the blue from a colleague working at a company that Don sometimes worked for. "Don," he said, "we're calling because we wanted to let you know that you earned a bonus this year."

This was unexpected but welcome news. Don said, "Great. How much will it be for?"

"Let me take a look." When he got back on the line, he said, "It's $28,300."

Don was speechless. This was the figure they needed to cover the adoption expenses for twins, and with $300 dollars to spare. There was a beat and then Don said, "Gonzalo, do you know what this means?"

"What?"

"This means that Grace and I are going to be getting twins."

On 21 August the adoption papers for twins were sent out to China. The Whites settled down for a long and nervous wait. It usually takes a considerable time to hear back, often years, and yet just seven days later, on 28 August, the agency called Don and Grace. They had received their list of children to be adopted. Top of the list were twin girls with cleft lips and palates. Their

Chinese Mandarin names translated as Elegant Cloud and Elegant Autumn. Did Don and Grace want to adopt them?

Grace insisted that they must first make sure that they were able to care for the children's needs properly, and so they began to research cleft-lip issues. The Whites also wanted to see how much they could find out about the girls' lives in China, but all they had to go on was the name of the girls' CWI. Then they found out that there were internet groups who swapped their experiences of travelling to China to collect their adoptive children, and there were sometimes details posted about the CWIs the children came from. So Grace sent out a request on the internet: "Does anybody know anything about a set of twins who were abandoned somewhere around 15 September 2003, and if you do please get back to us?"

About twelve hours later, they received a five-page email from Linda Shum, the same lady who had originally helped feed the twins when they were three days old. She was able to tell Grace about the girls right from the time they were found, through to driving them all the way to Beijing. She even had a video of the journey. She was also able to tell them about New Hope Foster Home and the girls' cleft-lip repair surgery in Shantou. She sent pictures of the babies, and gave them the number of Robin and Joyce. Feeling very excited, Don and Grace called China.

Robin and Joyce were limited by confidentiality issues, but they were thrilled to hear that the girls had been matched with possible parents. The Whites still had very little knowledge about cleft-affected children, but Robin and Joyce were very encouraging and helped Don and Grace understand what special issues the girls might need help with, and how the babies would make a full recovery after their surgeries.

The Whites hit it off immediately with Robin and Joyce. They were very excited to be in contact with people who knew the girls so well, and to see how the Hills were so committed to caring for the children in the home. The Hills' encouragement was just what they needed to give them the confidence to put themselves forward as the twins' new parents.

Soon, the Hills were able to send them up-to-date pictures of the twins – with their new, post-repair smiles.

The adoption papers went through in record time. Sometimes there can be significant delays before all the paperwork goes through, but only three months after applying to adopt them, Don and Grace went out to China to collect the girls. The Whites were also unusually fortunate in that they were allowed to collect the girls themselves from Robin and Joyce. In China, only the CWI where the children were originally placed may do the necessary paperwork for the adoption and carry out the handover to the parents, so most babies must travel back to their CWI for the actual adoption. But as Don had wide experience of speaking engagements in Asia and as they were travelling as a private couple, the Chinese Centre for Adoption Affairs decided to give them their kind permission to drop by New Hope Foster Home. Don says, "I do believe that God just intervened in a great way. I really do believe that tremendous favour was granted to us."

On 12 September, fifteen months after Sydney and Reagan were born, Grace and Don arrived at New Hope Foster Home to meet their daughters. Robin and Joyce gave them a tour of the home so that they could share something of the girls' early life, and Joyce chatted about the girls' little habits and personalities. The girls were too young to have anything explained to them, so to avoid any separation anxiety, Robin was careful to show the Whites around New Hope without the twins seeing them for a while.

Robin and Joyce's hope for all the children is for them to find their forever family. It is a wonderful day when this happens. But it is also a difficult day. It is sad for the nannies and for Rob and Joyce to have to say goodbye to children that they have cared for, for between one and three years. It is even more traumatic for the child: they are being taken away from the people they have bonded with and inexplicably handed over to strangers – from the babies' point of view, Joyce says, it looks more like a kidnap. But Robin and Joyce have worked out that the best thing to do is to get the children settled in with their new parents as quickly as possible, and with minimum fuss in parting.

So now, it was time for Grace and Don to meet the girls.

The girls were taking their afternoon nap on their mats in the spacious playroom. Robin asked Don and Grace to go in and pick the girls up and hold them as they woke up. Then Robin took a deep breath and said, "OK, we need you to leave now."

So without any fanfare, Don and Grace got into the car with their girls and waved a quiet goodbye to Robin and Joyce.

Once they were in the car and driving away, the girls both began to protest loudly. It was a very difficult moment for all concerned. Don says, "They just started crying and were very upset. They were like, 'We don't know what's happening. We don't know these people.' We tried to give them their bottles but they really didn't want that. But after thirty minutes or so, they sort of settled in, and by the time we got to our hotel in Beijing, I am not exaggerating when I say that it was as if they had been with us forever. Back in our room, we gave them their bottles and they had a nap in their cribs, and when they woke up they were our children."

When the White family got back to the States, life became very full on. There were all the expected issues of settling two active and opinionated young ladies of fifteen months into a house that had once been home to one well-organized, mid-life couple and two sedate dogs. But once everyone had got used to the new routine, and the girls had made friends with the dogs, got used to their new beds and thoroughly explored their new house, then the twins began to blossom.

Grace and Don began to see that there were many advantages in starting a family at their particular stage in life, since they had more than adequate time and resources to devote to their little package of double blessing and double fun and games. However, they were grateful to have the support of friends, especially those with young families, who brought round meals, shared child-rearing tips and techniques, or just joined together with the Whites in big family meals.

When they were eighteen months old, Sydney and Reagan had further surgery to close the palates in the roofs of their mouths. In October 2008, when they were five years old, the girls had their final surgery to help them form words, and then began to make fast progress with their speech.

The twins were very fortunate because they did not have any of the heart problems that can often accompany cleft palates. They had never suffered from the infant malnutrition that results from simply not being unable to suck and feed. Don says, "I now work with Love Without Boundaries, the organization that provided surgery for the twins, and have just got back from China where we have a cleft Healing Home, specifically designed to care for children with cleft lips and palates. We recently lost a child there who had had a very good repair, but who later had a heart attack. It is a much more common malady than people realize, for those cleft-affected babies who don't get help in time."

Joyce had explained to Don that the twins' surgery was

organized by Amy Eldridge through Love Without Boundaries, so as soon as Don was back home in America he had called Amy and found out all he could about their work. He insisted on paying for the girls' surgery, and was amazed to hear how little it had cost to make such a huge impact on the girls' lives.

Don is now on the Board of LWB and ardently committed to helping with the programmes that LWB run to deliver medical and nutritional help to children in CWIs, as well as education and foster care projects. Amy and LWB have since opened three cleft Healing Homes, to help more cleft babies get the kind of help that made such a difference to Sydney and Reagan.

Don and Grace have also travelled back to New Hope Foster Home and helped with a joint project that Amy and Joyce have put into place, to care for fragile children before and after surgery. The eighteen-bed Heartbridge unit in the extension at New Hope gives children the chance to make a full recovery after surgeries and to live a full and healthy life.

Some Mead Johnson's baby bottles, a lady willing to drive through the night, Joyce and Rob caring for fragile babies at their home, two doctors who travelled to share their skills, a couple offering to help build a playground and then being open to consider adoption; all these factors added together now mean that the Whites have two beautiful daughters, and the twins are growing up fit and healthy with their own mum and dad. Whether as bridesmaids, Christmas angels or rampaging around Disney World in matching sunglasses, Sydney and Reagan are a much-loved twin constellation of bright energy, each one precious and irreplaceable.

1 2

Ellie – a chance encounter

Let us love, not in word or speech, but in truth and action.

1 John 3:18 (NRSV)

Shortly after the twins arrived at the New Hope Foster Home, Joyce received a baby girl called Ellie. She was ten months old and in the early stages of heart failure. The main vessel leading out from her heart had an obstructive kink. With each beat, some of the out-flowing blood was pushed back into the heart, making it swell and weaken. Joyce put the baby on the right medication to keep her alive and began a search for help.

It was not a complicated operation for a heart surgeon: it would involve removing the kink in the main artery and rejoining it to the baby's heart, but Joyce needed to find a specialist who was used to working with the tiny heart of a baby. After six months of following up several leads that came to nothing, she still did not have a surgeon to help Ellie.

At the end of June 2004, Ellie stopped feeding and became so weak that she could not sit up. All she could take were tiny sips of water.

Joyce took Ellie in to Beijing United Hospital. The doctor examined the baby and checked her medication, but his conclusion was bleak. "Look," he said, "I can keep her here and put her on an intravenous drug to keep her heart going a little longer, but I'm going to give you a week to find a surgeon for her. Without surgery, this baby won't live."

As Joyce left the cool hospital building and went out into the warm summer's day, she thought, "I've tried for six months and found no one. How can I find someone in a week?"

Two months earlier, a youth pastor in Singapore had been reading about Ellie in Joyce's monthly newsletter. One of the people in his congregation was a surgeon. The pastor told him about the baby who desperately needed heart surgery.

"Do you think you could possibly help?" he asked.

"I'm sorry," he replied, "but your friend really needs a paediatric cardiac surgeon. I'm a general surgeon."

But the pastor's request stayed with him. A few weeks later the surgeon was standing in the arrivals hall at Singapore Airport, waiting to meet a friend. As he looked out across the arrivals hall he saw an Indian man who looked vaguely familiar. "I'm sure I know him," he thought. "I think I met him once in the hospital and he's a paediatric cardiac surgeon." So, feeling rather foolish, and hoping he had not made a mistake, he caught up with the man and asked if he was in fact a paediatric surgeon.

The man looked surprised but said, "Yes. That's right. I'm Dr Sriram Shankar."

"There's a lady in Beijing and she really needs your help," the surgeon blurted out. He proceeded to explain about baby Ellie and the urgent need to find someone to help with her heart surgery.

To his amazement, Dr Sriram took Joyce's details and agreed to contact her as soon as possible.

It was now four days since the doctor at the hospital had told Joyce that Ellie had just one week left to live. Another three days, and she would have to bring Ellie home from the hospital to die. When Joyce saw Dr Sriram's message come through in her email box that morning, she replied immediately with all Ellie's information, but the truth was, after so many failed leads, Joyce was not hopeful. Ellie was now fading away fast and she knew it was very unlikely that Dr Sriram would get back to her in time. There were so many details to organize before Ellie could travel out for surgery and hardly any time left to make all the arrangements.

As Joyce lay in bed early the next morning, with the sounds of the foster home kitchen staff beginning the day's preparations below, she said, "You know, Rob, I don't think we have a chance for this one."

Suddenly, Joyce's phone went off. A text message read, "Send baby now."

Joyce showed Rob the phone. His reaction was electric. He leapt out of bed, and minutes later, was racing down to the Singapore Embassy. Joyce already had Ellie's passport, but they were going to need a visa for the baby's specific travel dates.

But when Rob got to the embassy, it was not good news. The staff behind the desk explained that it would take them three days to get Ellie's visa completed.

"But we don't have three days," Rob said. "We need those papers now."

One of the ladies behind the desk looked at him and said, "Aren't you one of those people that run the foster home up in the North?"

"Yes."

"Hold on a minute," she said.

Twenty minutes later she came back. She was holding Ellie's visa.

The only tickets available that day for Joyce and Ellie to fly out to Singapore were business class, so Rob bought them. Joyce did not complain!

So just a couple of hours after waking up and saying she didn't think there was going to be any hope for Ellie's surgery, Joyce was madly packing a bag to fly out to Singapore. She rushed over to the hospital to pick up Ellie but found that the baby needed to stay attached to the medication pump that was keeping her alive, so she asked the hospital if she could carry the pump out with her. Somehow, Joyce got into the car with a very sick baby, an intravenous syringe driver that was still pumping away, and her own bulging and hastily packed bag.

But as they drove to the airport, it began to dawn on Joyce that she had not discussed with Rob or the Board how they were going to fund the surgery. She did not even know how much the surgery was going to cost. What she did know, however, was that there was no money in the account and that Ellie's costs could easily come to $50,000.

She got out her phone and called JT. She said, "JT, I've got Ellie here with me and I'm taking her to Singapore for her last-chance surgery. I don't know how much it is going to cost, but would you be prepared to underwrite the surgery?"

JT did not hesitate. He replied, "Just get the baby on the flight."

"But it could come to as much as thirty or even fifty thousand dollars," Joyce told him, anxiously.

"Just get her on the flight."

When Joyce arrived at Beijing Airport, she went to the business-class lounge and began putting a new syringe on the pump driver, ready to get on the plane. But then she noticed a pilot walking towards them. He stopped in front of Joyce and stared at the sick baby and the medical equipment. He introduced himself as the pilot for their flight to Singapore.

"Do you have medical clearance for this child to fly?" he asked.

"No," Joyce said, "but I can tell you this. If you don't let me on the flight, this child will die. If she doesn't get on, she doesn't have a chance."

"I'm sorry, but I can't let you get on the flight unless we have documented medical clearance."

"What will it take for you to let me on this flight?" Joyce said. "I am a doctor. Let me sign anything that you need me to sign."

The pilot looked at Joyce, and then he looked at the baby, and went away.

He came back carrying a blank sheet of A4 paper and handed it to Joyce.

"Just write something down and sign. Just write that you won't divert the flight if she dies."

"Divert the plane to where?" said Joyce. "She has nowhere else to go. She will either die here or live in Singapore – that's the only direction we are going."

"Just sign it."

So Joyce scribbled something down and signed.

By the time they boarded the flight Ellie had not eaten anything for four days. Her breathing was fast and shallow, and as Joyce looked down on the fuzz of baby hair and Ellie's closed eyes, she really did not know if Ellie was up to surviving the six-hour flight. All that was keeping the baby alive now was the medication in the intravenous pump.

As Joyce was changing the syringe once again, she looked up and was amazed to see JT walking down the aisle of the plane towards her.

"But I didn't know you were going to be on this flight!" said Joyce.

"I was already booked in for a business trip." He looked down at the baby Joyce was holding. "And so this is Ellie."

They arrived in Singapore some time before midnight. JT helped Joyce carry the syringe driver and all her bags off the plane and then got her in a taxi to the home of another friend and New Hope Board member.

Early next morning, Joyce took Ellie to the KK Women's and Children's Hospital. But as she got out of the taxi in front of the glass doors of the hospital, with the baby in her arms and the syringe driver still pumping away, she felt only too aware that she must look rather a sight, especially since, in the rush to get there, she had thrown on any old clothes and her hair had become as wild as it looked in her very un-favourite passport picture. She also felt anxious about explaining who she was to the staff and then having to try and find a doctor she had never met in a hospital she did not know.

She went inside the glass doors and looked around for which way to go. She saw two doctors walking down a flight of steps towards her. They looked at Joyce oddly and stopped.

"Are you Joyce from Beijing?" one of them said.

"Yes," she said, surprised they knew her name.

"My goodness, you got here pretty quickly. I'm Dr Sriram, the surgeon who is going to be operating on baby Ellie today. And this is my colleague who will be helping in the operation."

"You must have teleported yourself here," said the cardiologist.

By two o'clock that night, Ellie was in surgery. When she came round several hours later, she had whiskers of mucus down her face from her long ordeal and just wanted Joyce to hold her. But within a day she was looking much better, off her drips and busily tearing at the wrapper of a sweet given to her by one of the nurses. Joyce rang Robin and JT with the good news. Ellie was going to make a full recovery.

She could also tell them that the hospital had offered to fund all Ellie's surgery costs through their KK Regional Outreach to Kids Fund.

After a few days recuperating, Ellie was well enough to fly home to Beijing, where Joyce would continue to care for her until she was completely fit and strong.

Eighteen months later, some three years after being abandoned on the street – probably because her birth parents felt there was no help for the baby – Ellie left to join her new parents in Sweden. Every year the family still send back photos to Robin and Joyce of a little girl with a square-cut fringe and a huge cheeky grin, growing up healthy and strong, and surrounded by the love of her own forever family.

13

A phone call for help

We can't help everyone, but everyone can help someone.
Dr Loretta Scott

In June 2004, Joyce was thrilled to hear that nine more babies had been approved as being healthy enough to go forward for adoption. She took great pleasure in being able to move their little photos over into the "waiting to be adopted" column on her office board. The children were all growing fast, and Joyce had recently set up a preschool to meet the needs of the babies as they turned into active little people, ready to learn new things, but it would be good for them to move to be with their new families as soon as possible.

With the extension to the new home completed, the Hills were looking forward to a time when they could consolidate, make sure everything was running really well, and perhaps even catch their breath a little.

But one morning, Joyce was working in the office when a call came through that left her deeply distressed. A lady had been visiting a CWI and had seen great need there among dying children. She had never met Joyce, but someone had told her that Joyce had a home where she was taking care of sick children. Please, she asked, could Joyce do something to help?

Joyce and Robin were shocked to realize what was happening. They sat in the office talking about what they could do to help these dying babies. Up to that point, their mission statement had been to save children who were treatable. Should they now begin to try and reach children who had been abandoned because they were dying, or who had been sent home from hospitals as untreatable, and then found their way to the CWI?

It was hard to understand how a parent would not take home a dying child and comfort them, but the Hills knew that among other cultural pressures, the fear of a death in the house is very powerful in poor and traditional families. There are ancient cultural taboos, dating back thousands of years, about how unlucky it is for a family to have a child die in the house. Even at the Banpo Museum where one can see the excavation of a 4,000-year-old Chinese village, it is clear that deceased children were buried far away from the main village.

"Should we divert resources to go down this road?" Rob said. "Is this a door that God is opening, because it's a major thing?"

But while they were considering how to help, Joyce received a second distraught phone call. The same lady had just seen another dying child in need, and this time had asked the CWI staff to let her take the baby.

"Please can you do something to help her?" she said.

Robin and Joyce went to visit the CWI, and they were allowed to bring Rebekah back to New Hope. But when Joyce examined the baby's physical condition and assessed her needs, she saw that Rebekah was going to require help from specialist surgeons to build a working bladder and reconstruct her pelvis bones. It would be very expensive surgery indeed – something a poor family could never hope to afford.

But when people heard about Rebekah, the funds to give the

baby a new chance were quickly in place. Joyce's old classmate Ling, who had a passion to help the baby girl when she heard about her in the newsletter, raised substantial funds. The Australian Chinese Medical Association donated towards hospital costs, and surgeons in Sydney agreed to take on Rebekah's long and complicated surgery and waive their fees.

It was now a race to get Rebekah's passport and paperwork ready, and above all, to bring the baby up to her correct weight so that she could cope with the demands of surgery. By the end of October, just three months after Rebekah had been taken from a darkened room and brought to New Hope Foster Home, the baby was well enough to travel with Joyce to Sydney for bladder reconstruction.

Joyce waited anxiously as Rebekah went under the anaesthetic for the long and difficult operation. Through the seven hours of waiting, Joyce became increasingly anxious for the baby. She walked round the hospital with a pager on her hip, then sat in the waiting room but found she could not stay still, so walked around the hospital some more. Finally, she was allowed to go into the recovery room. When she saw Rebekah, Joyce began to weep with relief to see that the baby had survived.

"This is not your daughter, is she? Why are you crying?" said the anaesthetist.

But Joyce just shook her head. She did not have the words to explain – no, this baby was not her daughter. Rebekah had no mother to pace the floor and to weep tears of relief, but in her place Joyce had been given the honour of being this child's mother for a short time, to pace and worry and weep for her when there was no one else to do so. Rebekah had been given up for dead, but now she was on the way to being healed. Joyce knew that she had been given a precious gift, to witness God's love for Rebekah.

In spite of some temporary bowel complications, Rebekah went on to make a full recovery with a complete reconstruction of all her female organs. Rebekah would stay on at New Hope Foster Home for the following three years, and in that time she grew into a very distinct little personality. With her thick, straight-cut fringe and pigtails, she was always ready to get busy with life's discoveries, as she drew pictures of her nannies and herself in the preschool or ran to get on the swings in the play park.

The bouncy little girl who later left New Hope on a spring day in 2007 was hard to connect with the swaddled and dying scrap that arrived from the CWI in Henan three years before. Rebekah became the much-loved daughter of her own mother and father in Sweden.

Robin and Joyce realized that if they were going to save more children like Rebekah – children who had once been classed as terminal and hopeless cases – then they needed to have a permanent presence in the CWI so that they could be ready to help the babies as soon as they came in.

So Joyce decided to try a direct approach. Feeling very nervous, she travelled to Jiaozuo to talk to the director of the CWI. She had a radical proposal: if he would let her take over the rooms with the terminally sick children, then she would undertake to not only completely renovate the rooms but also support the costs involved in running a fully resourced palliative care unit.

The director was very taken aback. He could not understand why Joyce would want to get so involved with dying children.

"Do you want to experiment on these children?" he asked her.

Joyce said, no, she did not want to carry out any experiments, but as a doctor, she wanted to support the CWI by offering hospice care for the very sick children, and also offer any medical help she could find, to see if some children could be saved.

"All we are asking you for is an empty floor that we could renovate and put a few beds in to look after the children that you feel are dying."

It was a bold move for the director, but he decided to give Joyce permission to go ahead.

She phoned Rob immediately with the news of their "gift", permission to set up a unit to care for the dying children in the CWI. They would be caring for babies who were either very premature, or who had severe birth defects that were not compatible with prolonged life.

As soon as she got back to Beijing they called a meeting with the Board. Joyce's question to its members was: was it right to divert their resources to children who were often not going to make it? But they all agreed that if they could save just one life in the special care unit, then they should do it. One of the Board members agreed immediately to underwrite the $20,000 cost of the refurbishment.

They would also need to source a permanent staff member on site to look after the day-to-day running of the unit and nannies to care for the babies.

It would be a difficult and sensitive project on all levels, and the Hills knew they would need everyone's prayers. Joyce and Robin were also aware that it was going to be hard emotionally, to care for babies specifically sent to them because they were classified as dying. They were willing to fight for those babies to have a chance, but they knew that not all the children would make it. They decided together that their hope for the children would be, "To comfort always, to relieve often, and to save sometimes."

* * *

In July 2004, Robin and Joyce moved into the family cottage that Rob had built next to the main home in the style of a traditional, one-storey *hutong* house, with three sides looking into a central garden area. He also installed a little plunge pool in the courtyard garden, where the foster children would enjoy playing during the hot summer months. Rob left the wooden roof-beams exposed inside so that the rooms were spacious and full of character. Joyce's only stipulation had been an indoor water fountain in the entrance lobby, in the style of the Malaysian houses from her childhood. This turned out to be the perfect place for Katie to keep her terrapin collection.

The new extension was now also completed, giving space to care for twice as many babies. A long sunny corridor ran the length of all the rooms, its polished bamboo floors gleaming in the sun. On the wall of the new entrance lobby, one of Joyce's quilts spelled out the word "Hope" next to plaques and good wishes from Western and Chinese friends and supporters. People visiting the Home for the first time often remarked on the friendly, peaceful atmosphere that met them as they came through the glass doors into the welcoming entrance hall. Sooner or later a royal little procession of three of four toddlers would appear, making their way slowly and thoughtfully from their playroom to the dining room, pausing every so often to look round or to just stop and have a think, then ushered on by their nannies to follow the delicious smell of dumplings into the dining-room, where lunch was served up by their friend the cook, beaming away under his splendid white hat.

The Hills knew the children needed to feel that all the adults in the home were kind and could be trusted. Prominently placed in the hallway was a large pin-board, with photos of all staff, kitchen workers, cleaners, nannies and staff directors – showing that the home valued every person working at New Hope as part of a team.

In May, the Hills welcomed Marsha on staff, and she became one of their secret weapons in locating and helping sick children from CWIs all over China. Whether it was obtaining tickets for airlines at short notice, ordering complicated medical equipment, or negotiating regulations and visas, Marsha got it sorted. While they were still thinking about whether they could face starting over again, it had been Marsha who had begun sending them babies with heart conditions – babies who needed to have special care if they were to survive.

Marsha was a Beijinger, energetic and practical with a big smile and a bouncy ponytail, always willing to go the extra mile, and many more, to help children in China. After an English degree, Marsha worked for an American called Tim Baker who was caring for babies in a foster home in Lang Fang. When certain CWIs had a new child with severe medical needs they would often phone Marsha to see if she could find help for them, and Marsha found that she was contacting Joyce for medical advice on a regular basis. So in 2004 Joyce and Rob asked her if she might like to take on a full-time post as project coordinator for New Hope Healing Home.

Marsha found that she soon felt part of the family at Hope and became firm friends with Robin and Joyce. She says, "I'd been watching them and I saw Robin and Joyce show the same respect to a college graduate as to a farmer. I saw a real love for Chinese people, not just for the children."

The team of people drawn together by the same wish, to help a tiny but irreplaceable child, went a long way beyond the walls of the New Hope building. People all over the world read Joyce's newsletters, followed the progress of the children, and contributed funds, formula, baby clothes and medication. Doctors emailed Joyce to let her know that they were willing to help out with surgeries, and volunteers from across the world came to stay and help out with vital jobs such as travelling with a child who might need to fly to Hong Kong or Singapore for surgery, or helping out in the preschool. Volunteers also brought over essential supplies of things hard to find in China.

One of the more unusual donations given to Robin and Joyce was three large Mongolian yurts, complete with several beds and pretty wall hangings. They were set up on the land at the back of the house, and allowed groups of up to twenty volunteers to stay at the home. As well as falling in love with all the babies, the volunteers enjoyed visiting the Great Wall or the ancient Forbidden City in Beijing – although a visit to the newly opened Starbucks was also very popular.

The Hills drew up some volunteer guidelines to help visitors fit in culturally. For example, it is not legal to talk to the nannies about faith issues. There were also special medical issues that visitors needed to take on board, as the majority of the children were recovering from surgery and vulnerable to infections, so procedures like hand-washing rules are a must for all visitors.

Joyce found that most volunteers could be trusted to fit in responsibly with the children's needs and were a great help. Less helpful were new volunteers who upset the nannies by giving them conflicting advice.

Rob also admits ruefully, "We feel that it can sometimes be the case that we have helpers who come here to be helped."

The babies kept to a Mediterranean routine in summer, with a long siesta during the heat of the day, napping on mats in the air-conditioned playrooms. As the late afternoon grew cooler, the nannies could take the babies out for walks to the village where the children made friends with groups of grannies who came out to chat in the village square beneath the little loudspeaker tower. They waved to grandpas watering rows of maize in tiny cottage gardens, or watched the families sitting beneath the bamboo pergolas that seemed far too rickety to support the magnificent orange gourds hanging in swathes of blue net.

In August, Robin, Joyce and the children travelled to Bali for the wedding of Rob's daughter Natasha. She looked stunning in her flowing white dress, her blonde hair swept up under a veil. All the family came to celebrate together, from Australia, Hong Kong, the USA and South America. It was wonderful to spend time together and it was also a chance for Robin and Joyce to rest, after what had been a very hectic and exhausting year.

14

Teresa

Until he extends the circle of his compassion to all living things, man will not himself find peace.

EDWARD EVERETT HALE

When they got back, the Hills were pleased to see that work on the special care unit at Rebekah's CWI was progressing well. Meanwhile, at New Hope they were beginning to care for several very sick children from there, originally destined to pass away as hopeless cases. Teresa was one of these babies, arriving at New Hope four weeks after Rebekah.

Teresa had spina bifida. A large purple swelling bulged out from her lower back where the base of her spine had failed to close. She was a tiny, stick-like child, and had to sleep curled up on her front because of the lump on her back. When Teresa arrived at New Hope Foster Home, Joyce laid her down on her examination table in the office to assess her medical needs and saw that the child needed surgery very fast. As the swelling increased and put pressure on the nerves, Teresa was at increasing risk of becoming paralysed and unable to walk.

Dr Jorge Lazareff was Director of Paediatric Surgery at Mattel Children's Hospital at UCLA in America. He spent much of his time and expertise operating on children free of charge in many countries around the world. He had already arranged to make a trip out to China and offered to also include Teresa with other neurosurgeries he had scheduled. Joyce was relieved to have such a competent and caring surgeon coming to Teresa's aid.

Before the operation, Dr Lazareff gently held the baby on his shoulder, ready to assess her situation, addressing her as "little Teresita", which is the diminutive used for "Teresa" in his Spanish family. She was not able to lie flat against his chest since the swelling was pulling her back tightly. By now the swelling on her lower back was the size of a large orange, and a dark, bruised colour. She had a look of puzzled patience in her almond-shaped eyes.

After a delicate and long operation, Joyce was able to visit Teresa, now back in her hospital cot and recovering well. The baby had tubes taped to her mouth and a wad of cloth placed under her tummy to keep her from rolling onto the dressing, but her back was now perfectly flat, the nerves safely closed inside a flap of skin. Teresa could now grow with every chance of walking.

But once the spinal sack is closed in, there is an increase in pressure along the spinal fluid and into the brain. The remedy is to place a tube or shunt in the brain to drain excess fluid off through the chest and into the abdomen. Very rarely, this can become blocked or infected and needs to be replaced.

Some time after Dr Lazareff returned to the USA, Teresa began to show symptoms of having a blockage in her shunt. Brain fluid began to seep from the shunt's point of insertion and Joyce took her into a local hospital to arrange to have it changed.

But the hospital administration insisted that they could not allow one of their doctors to operate on Teresa. They said that Joyce must ask the American doctor to return and carry out the repair. After much pleading from Joyce, the doctors removed the shunt but refused to replace it with a new one. They stapled shut the wound in Teresa's scalp and discharged her.

Joyce took Teresa home and tried to find someone to help her, but after two weeks pressure began to build inside the baby's head and the wound began to rupture. As pressure continued to build, Joyce could see brain matter beginning to push through the wound.

Joyce was now desperate. She sent off an email and photographs to Dr Lazareff. She explained that the local hospitals would not replace the defective shunt.

"Please come," she wrote, "otherwise this child will die."

It was late November and in the USA everyone was going home for Thanksgiving weekend, but Dr Lazareff agreed to return to Beijing to operate on Teresa. All flights were packed for the holiday, but somehow he managed to find plane tickets.

But they still needed to register Dr Lazareff to get clearance for him to operate in China, and that would take time. And Joyce needed to get a hospital to agree to take Teresa's case.

"By some miracle," Joyce said, "I managed to get him registered here with the American hospital. It's never an easy thing to do. I pleaded with them: 'Just one case, to save this child's life. Please, just take her in and keep her pain free until the surgeon can get here.'"

So Teresa was admitted to the American hospital to prepare her for surgery. But while Joyce was driving home in the car – and just as Dr Lazareff was to leave the USA for China – she got a call on her mobile. It was the paediatrician at the American hospital. "We've just done a CT scan and we can see brain tissue coming through the skull," she informed Joyce. "Tell your surgeon not to come. It's too late."

Joyce had seen the brain matter extruding with her own eyes before Teresa was admitted. She already knew that Teresa's case was desperate. She had taken Teresa to hospital hoping something could be done for her against all odds. But she was now emotionally exhausted, and had just been told that it was entirely hopeless. She agreed to tell Dr Lazareff not to come.

But Joyce found that she could not make herself call his number. Dr Lazareff was Teresa's only chance of living. She could not make a call that would stop him coming and cancel Teresa's last hope.

So the next evening Joyce picked up Dr Lazareff from Beijing Airport. He slept, and in the morning, he operated on Teresa again.

The operation was a complete success. Teresa made a full recovery and had no more difficulties with her shunt. She went back to live with Joyce and her nannies at New Hope Foster Home. Eventually she was well enough to be placed on the adoption register at her original CWI, where she had once been considered too fragile to live.

In 2007 Kelly and Karen Hansen were enjoying life and feeling very content. This is their story.

> *We had a nice marriage and three beautiful daughters. We enjoyed our jobs and church, and spent a lot of family time together. There was no reason to make any changes. Our third daughter had been adopted from China and we thought that we might go back someday for another child, but there was no hurry.*
>
> *I always often looked through the web pages with pictures and stories of children who were orphaned, but I wasn't looking for another child.*
>
> *Then it happened. A picture of a little girl appeared on the screen, and tears came to my eyes. I didn't read*

Joyce and Robin's wedding.

Joyce and Robin with Katie in their first foster home.

The staff at Hope Foster Home in Beijing.

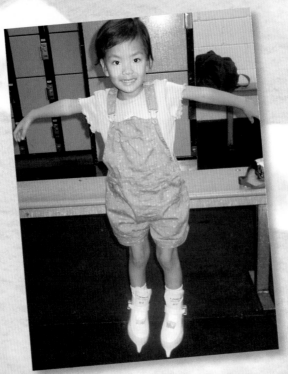

Bethany on ice skates.

New Hope Foster Home.

Toby after foot surgery, and living with his forever family.

A stroll in the village.

Inside New Hope Foster Home.

Sydney and Reagan after cleft palate surgery, and with their forever family.

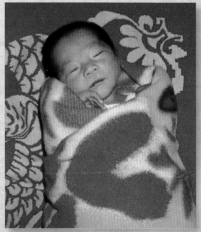

Rebekah on arrival, and with Amber.

Dr Lazareff with Teresa.

Teresa.

Liz Kulp having just collected Howie – a wonderful picture of a new mum and her son.

Hadassa feeding William.

The suitcase bed.

William with Marcus, a volunteer.

Steven and Mary Beth Chapman and family – Emily is secon

Maria's Big House of Hope.

from left: Aron, Adrian, Ruth, Amber, Kaitlyn,

her name or about her medical conditions. I got up and walked away from my computer. I knew this child was supposed to be mine.

I called my wife and told her to look at the website. I didn't tell her about how I had felt. Later that day I told her what had happened, and asked her to pray about this child. We had never considered adopting a child with spina bifida. On the medical conditions checklist for our first adoption, we said that we would not accept a child with such a serious medical condition, but we wanted to be open to the will of God.

With hesitation, we started the process. But what we feared has turned into a great blessing. Our daughter was left at an orphanage due to her medical needs. The Lord saved her by placing her in the paths of people serving God and orphans in China. They arranged for her to have several surgeries, and with the Lord's hand, her life was saved. She is truly a miracle baby. We cannot imagine our family without her. We thank God every morning when our little girl comes running to us with her big smile and says, "I love you, Mummy and Daddy." We adopted "an older child with severe medical needs". We came home with the daughter God had chosen for us from the day she was born.

Kelly and Karen sent this note to Joyce and Robin, along with photos of Teresa swimming in the sea, camping, abseiling and playing in the garden with her three sisters and her impossibly young-looking parents. Teresa's elegant little face is no longer serious with pain, but relaxed and happy, and she smiles out confidently at whatever life has in store.

15

Tiffany

*To every thing there is a season, and a time for every
purpose under heaven: A time to be born, and a time
to die… a time to weep, and a time to laugh; a time to
mourn, and a time to dance.*

ECCLESIASTES 3:1–2, 4 (KJV)

Since Joyce had been given the go ahead to open a palliative
and special care unit in Rebekah's former CWI, Rob had been
making the long journey to Jiaozuo every few weeks to supervise
the renovations for the special care unit on the sixth floor. During
that time it had changed from a run-down, dark part of the
building to a newly painted suite of rooms with a blond wood
floor and cheerful murals on the walls.

By the end of Chinese New Year the renovated floor was fully
fitted out with cots and incubators, and Joyce was able to tell the
director that they were ready to take in the first babies. She had
agreed with the CWI that they would take in children who were
less than three years old, small enough to fit in the cots, and who
were in need of special care. They waited for the CWI staff to send
up those sick and dying children that they thought should have a
place in the unit.

But nothing happened.

When Joyce and Robin went into the director's office to sign the contract for how things were to proceed, he informed them that all funds and control of the unit must now be placed in his hands. He would pick and train the staff himself. Permission for the unit was withdrawn unless Joyce complied.

But Joyce knew that if she was not able to direct the unit on the same lines as the New Hope Foster Home in Beijing, with the same principles and standard of care, then it would be a pointless exercise with no change for the children in the CWI.

"I'm sorry," said Joyce, "but that's not according to our policy. We have already discussed this and we hire and fire and train our own nannies. This unit will be run the same way as we run the home in Beijing."

There was a complete stand off. The director refused to listen. But neither was Joyce giving in. She told him that if he insisted, he could take over the unit, but she could no longer continue. "Then I will remove all my cribs and incubators and oxygen tanks, and you will have a floor of nicely renovated rooms, but you must take care of the children yourself," Joyce told him.

She could not believe what she was saying. They had already spent $20,000 of funds, funds donated specifically to renovate the rooms on the sixth floor of the CWI. She stood there thinking, "What am I going to tell the donors? I'm walking away and have just blown $20,000 of their own generous money."

But she knew the unit would serve no purpose unless run on the same principles as the home in Beijing – to treat all the children as if they were their own. There was a terrible moment while she waited for the director's response.

"OK," he said finally. "Have it your way. You can go ahead and look after the unit."

Feeling very shaky and exhausted after what had almost

happened, Joyce went back to the unit to recover. She says, "I knew that I had to stand my ground as to the quality of care the children would receive. All I knew was that God had everything in control and I was given favour to care for the children the way they deserved to be cared for."

So the babies began to arrive from the main CWI building on the five floors below. In the first four weeks the special care unit was open, twelve children considered to be dying came up from the floors below, and three of those babies passed away with carefully administered pain relief and the loving comfort of their nannies.

But if a baby had any chance of recovering with the right medical help, then they were transferred north to New Hope Foster Home in Beijing. And each time a child left to be helped, their bed in the unit would be given to another child in need of extra care or feeding, or to a child too sick for any further treatment who needed palliative care.

Soon all twelve beds were filled in the SCU and five babies from the unit had been moved to live in Beijing in the hope that they would be able to get the medical help they needed to live – and one day, perhaps, be well enough to be adopted.

When premature triplets – two girls and a boy – arrived in the special unit, they caused a great stir. Their family were still in contact, but the triplets were in need of careful nursing to get them strong enough to go home. The shocked family came to the unit in rotations to help feed them and began to bond with them. With so many newborns to care for, Joyce was fast running out of the tiny diapers for premature babies that were so hard to find in China, and she put out a request for them in the list of needs kept in the newsletter.

April 2005 showed Beijing and the surrounding countryside

at its most delightful with magnolia, peach, plum and cherry in full flower. The weather was sunny and warm but not yet too hot. It also brought news for Ellie – the little girl who had been saved by a chance encounter of two surgeons in an airport. Ellie's parents would be arriving soon to take her home to Sweden.

Ellie, Teresa and Rebekah were all testaments to the Hills' belief that every child deserved every possible chance of life; that every child was infinitely precious. However, Joyce and Robin were only too aware that many of the babies who came would be too ill to be saved. The hope for these children was to hold and comfort them so that they could slip away without the physical distress of untreated pain or the emotional pain of being left alone.

Joyce's instinct was always to be ready to fight for each child until there was no last chance left to be uncovered. But over the three years that followed, she was to learn painful lessons about how long to fight for a child, and how to recognize that it was time to stop and prepare for a loving and peaceful end for a dying child.

Tiffany arrived at the SCU in Jiaozuo when she was just one day old. She had a severe spinal defect, and had lost the use of her legs. After her spinal opening was closed she had a shunt inserted internally to drain the excess fluid in her brain. But over the following eight months, Joyce had to send Tiffany for three operations to correct shunt blockages and the baby also suffered from repeated bouts of pneumonia.

Joyce was devastated when she saw that Tiffany's shunt was blocked for a fourth time and had to send the baby to hospital for yet another operation. But when Tiffany came out, she continued to have further problems.

Joyce agonized over whether to put the baby through yet more surgery. It seemed logical to stop, and yet Tiffany would look straight at Joyce and reach to take her fingers in her small grasp. She seemed to just keep fighting to live. Tiffany, along with another very sick child, was admitted to Beijing United Hospital to have her shunt replaced again.

One of the paediatricians there was a trained palliative care physician. As Joyce stood by Tiffany's bed, trying to decide what to do next, and trying to make that decision as if she were Tiffany's mother, the doctor approached her.

"Joyce," he said, "you realize you cannot save these two children. You have to decide when there is a limit to what you can do." Joyce listened while the doctor explained that she needed to call an ethics committee together in the hospital to help her decide what was best, as this was a difficult decision that she could not make on her own.

But then Tiffany rallied and gave everyone hope for several more weeks. But by October, she was once again back in hospital.

It did not seem fair to put the baby through any more surgery. In spite of high doses of medication, Tiffany could not shake off her brain and chest infections. She was dying.

But the grief of having to say goodbye to a cherished child, who had been fought for over so many months, took its toll both on Joyce and Robin and on the nursing staff and nannies. Tiffany was taken to the palliative care unit in Jiaozuo and given her own day and night nannies so that she did not have to go through the stress of being alone as she faded away. Joyce prescribed the right medical dosage to relieve any pain. Tiffany continued to fight on for several more months, loved and cared for by her nannies, but after repeated bouts of pneumonia, she died.

Joyce felt deeply sad. Of all the children that Joyce had taken in at New Hope, Tiffany had made her face what it meant to take care of fragile children on the edge of life. She was realizing that it was a very fine line indeed, between fighting against all odds to save a child, and recognizing the right of a dying child to die with peace and loving care. And this process was something that would happen again and again and again.

Joyce wrote in the newsletter: "Please pray for the work in the new Special Care Unit. This is a place where life-and-death decisions are made for the babies and it is never easy, both physically and emotionally for our staff."

Joyce and Rob agreed that their guiding principle for making palliative care decisions should be exactly as if each child were their own.

"Basically," says Joyce, "we ask, if it were our daughter or son, what would we do? How many shunts would we change? How many surgeries would we do before we say, 'That's enough'? How much suffering do you want to put this child through?"

Joyce and Rob did not have an ethics committee to help them make such decisions. They were the ethics committee. However, as a doctor, Joyce knew that she did not have to take medical decisions completely alone, since she had built up a wide network of specialist doctors who were willing to help her assess a child's chance of survival. A Hong Kong neurological specialist helped her to look through brain scans for another child and confirmed that they showed hardly any brain tissue left. Together they made the decision for that child: "No more shunts. Just let him go."

Joyce also attended palliative care conferences in Singapore. However, a great deal of the conferences focused on how the doctor might help parents make such decisions, but, Joyce explains, "Rob and I are the mothers and fathers. We have to make the decisions for each child and cope with the grieving, along with the nannies who care for the children each day."

Even though some of the children sent to the palliative care unit were so sick that they could live only a few days, Joyce would always give them a name and note their passing away in the newsletters that went out via the internet.

It was a hard fact, that opening one's heart to a large and growing family of children meant opening one's heart to the possibility that not all those children would make it through to a long life. Each decision to let a dying child go was the cause of grieving among their nannies and for Joyce.

After Tiffany's death, a volunteer painted a landscape of mountains and flowers along the garden wall outside the Hills' house. Halfway along the wall, a moon gate opening leads through into an orchard – where the children go to pick peaches in the summer. The name of every child that has passed away is written on the wall, among the painting of mountains and flowers, each name constantly visible from the windows of the Hills' house.

* * *

In July, Rob took a call from Australia. His eldest daughter Natasha, who had been married for only eleven months and had just given birth to her own little girl, had died of a brain aneurism.

She was a beautiful, healthy young woman and there had been absolutely no warning before her sudden death. Grief stricken, Rob and Joyce went home to attend his daughter's funeral and to comfort her husband and child.

16

William

It's not what you look at that matters, it's what you see.
ALBERT SCHWEITZER

In early 2004, while Joyce and Robin were beginning to try and help children like Rebekah, two sisters called Hadassah and Anna, then aged seventeen and twenty-three, were spending three weeks volunteering in that same CWI.

The girls were allowed to help the nannies care for some of the babies diagnosed as dying. When they got to the end of the corridor and went into the room to meet the babies for the first time they found nine babies, all deemed too hopeless to live or who needed much more input than was available. The long-term volunteers there suggested that the girls each pick out a child to care for.

Hadassah noticed an extremely tiny baby who had just been brought in. He had been born very prematurely and half of his hair had been shaved away. He was so thin that the bones showed through his skin and his face was wrinkled up like a little old man's. Hadassah says that at that time he looked like the least beautiful baby she had ever seen. "And yet I had to hold back tears as I watched him. He couldn't even cry because he was so weak. He would wrinkle his face and make a raspy noise that you could barely hear – which was the only way we knew he was crying. That's when I knew he was for me. And maybe that's everyone's reaction to a baby who needs help, but I knew that the feeling I had was from the Father's aching heart."

Hadassah asked for the baby's name, but he did not have one. He had been found under a bridge by a farmer and given to the police, who then brought him in to the CWI. As was usual, his photo had gone into the local paper for two weeks – but no one came to collect him.

The girls were allowed to think of a name for him. They gave him a name shared by royalty – William.

Hadassah asked if she could pick him up and feed him. But there was a problem. Baby William was too weak to take a feed. One of the volunteers fetched a cleft-palate bottle that she had brought in her supplies and Hadassah gently force-fed William by squeezing formula into his mouth until he swallowed it. She also noticed that his skin was a strange yellow colour. Someone mentioned that a baby with jaundice had yellow skin and also told her that the cure was sunlight, so every chance she got, Hadassah went over to the window and held William in the light.

The baby's skin was very cold and clammy to touch. Anna, Hadassah's sister, knew how serious this was – their brother's skin had been equally cold to the touch in the moments before he passed away after a long fight with cancer. But it was hard to know how to keep the baby warm. They got hold of some Chinese glass hot-water bottles and filled them with warm water. Then they wrapped William up inside a bundle of blankets with the well-padded bottles alongside, and tied it all up with string so that his strange bed did not fall apart. The girls took it in turns to carry on giving him feeds, holding their fragile package with great care.

At night, William had to go back to the room for the terminal babies, but the girls found out that no one was allowed to visit him. William would not get his tiny two-hourly feeds. But he was so cold to touch and he looked so sickly that the girls were afraid he might not last through the night, so Hadassah asked a worker to let her keep William in her room. Very reluctantly, the worker agreed.

It was a long and exhausting night. Anna and Hadassah took turns to get up and feed the starving baby. And they had a problem finding somewhere to put him. So they improvised, using a small, open suitcase, padded out with blankets. William settled comfortably into his little bed, although even in a small suitcase he looked minute, swaddled in the middle of his covers.

From that night on, the suitcase became his regular bed and Hadassah spent all her time with William, except when he was napping or taken away to see a doctor. Everyone in the volunteer team fell in love with the tiny baby and helped to rock him and walk him around. However, Anna found the experience of caring for a baby so near to death very hard at times, as she was old enough to have clear memories of when their brother died, but as she walked William up and down the corridor one day, she was filled with a sense of peace that God was looking after His children, no matter how long or short their lives.

William began to put on a little weight. He seemed stronger and began to look around with some curiosity, but now their three weeks were up and it was time for Anna and Hadassah to go back home. Hadassah rang her mother Lorrie in America. She told her that they had found the most wonderful baby. "I think you should adopt William, Mommy," Hadassah told her. "You said it was quiet in the house now, and William would make it loud."

Their mother assumed the girls were joking. She reminded them that she was now fifty. "Why don't you adopt him, then?"

Lorrie asked them.

But Lorrie's heart went out to William as she learned more about him. "I wish I could adopt him," she emailed back to Hadassah, "but I don't know how."

As they packed to leave, Hadassah and Anna were aware that many of the babies in that room had died during their stay. Hadassah held William tight and sang and prayed for him, and asked the long-term volunteers, Michelle, Hope and Emily, to take good care of him.

When they got home, the family was able to keep in touch via email and hear about William's progress. But Emily and the other volunteers noticed that William was getting weaker again, so they continued with the small night feeds – he needed the calories to stay alive. Emily says that she will never forget his fighting spirit. "He seemed so tough for such a tiny guy."

As the long-term volunteers' stay also came to an end, Lorrie knew they had to do something more to keep William alive, so she began to search for help for him. Through a friend she heard about Joyce and immediately emailed her, to explain her worries for William, and ask if Joyce could find a bed for him at New Hope.

Joyce replied to say that she would like to take William, but it was sadly the case that all their cots were full. So Lorrie got straight back to say that that was not a problem: since William was in a four-to-a-cot situation, it would be a step up for him if they could just find him his own drawer or shoebox – he took up so little room.

Joyce emailed back and said she would send her husband to get William. Rob made the eleven-hour journey and brought back not only William but also two other babies who needed feeding. Emily and the other volunteers travelled back with him on the train to help care for the babies.

William was two months old when he arrived at New Hope – according to the estimated birth date given him when he was found. Lorrie arranged to sponsor his expenses, and when he was three months, she managed to travel to China and visit New Hope. Joyce handed her a fat, cuddly butterball and for a moment Lorrie wondered if she had the wrong child. Joyce had taken wonderful care of William, including nursing him through spells where his throat would collapse and he would turn blue and pass out. At one point his heart had stopped and Joyce had had to resuscitate him.

Lorrie, along with her husband Brad, would have loved to adopt William and she looked into every possibility, but she found out that there is no mechanism whereby one can adopt a particular child. William might go on the adoption register at his CWI, but he would have to go through the open process and then would most likely be adopted by someone else. Lorrie tried to accept that she could not be William's mother.

William was now healthy enough for Joyce to arrange for him to live with a foster family close to the home, and he settled in well to village life.

Then when William was two and a half, Lorrie got some news from Joyce. William had been recalled back to his CWI ready to be adopted. This was wonderful news, but it meant that Lorrie and the family had to come to terms with the fact that they could never be the ones to adopt William and bring him home.

Joyce was quite surprised that William had been placed on the main adoption register, since children with mild special needs are not normally included. She queried whether he was on the correct register – he had mild coordination delay as a result of being born so prematurely – but the CWI were adamant that this was the right register for William.

Over the following year, Lorrie and Brad were able to visit William one last time while he was waiting at his old CWI for his new family to pick him up. But in the two weeks since he had left his New Hope foster family, William had changed a lot. His head had been shaved and his eyes were looking down at the floor. For a second time Lorrie almost failed to recognize William – till he gave her his unmistakable frown and smile.

William's new mum came to China to pick him up. But when she met the two-year-old with his big dark eyes full of curiosity, but still needing his walker, she was very taken aback. She was a nurse and realized that he had some special needs. She told the CWI that she had already adopted a child with special needs and did not feel able to offer the personal resources to care for a second.

She somehow got hold of Joyce's number and phoned her in floods of tears to explain how she felt unable to proceed. Joyce reassured the lady that it was OK for her to not take William if she felt unable to manage. (Some time later Joyce heard that the CWI had been able to match the lady with another child, and that adoption went ahead.)

Joyce was very sad to hear that William's adoption had fallen through. She asked his CWI if he could come back to live at New Hope, and sent some young volunteers with the home's driver on the day-long journey to fetch him.

Usually, a child with mild cerebral palsy would not be put forward for adoption by their CWI, but now William had all his adoption papers ready to go. Sadly, it is also the case that if an adoption is disrupted, that child will never have another chance of being put forward for adoption. William seemed to have missed his only chance to ever have his own family.

But Lorrie went ahead and made one last application through official channels to adopt a little boy. There is a very strict rule that prospective parents cannot request to adopt a specific child, and so she could not ask for William, but somehow his papers came through at the adoption agency in the USA.

When William was three and a half, he went home to his own forever family. Hadassah and Anna were now his own big sisters, and Lorrie and Brad were his mum and dad. Joyce was overjoyed. She says, "To me this is one of the crazy miracles that God had bestowed on that family and William – though the process was a bit convoluted."

At Christmas time in 2009, Lorrie sent Joyce their family newsletter, plus a wonderful picture of all the family taken on the beach at Anna's wedding, with William in his smart pink bow-tie, at the centre of his large and loving family. Lorrie told Joyce, "William has a sweet contagious smile and loves life, his family and all his big brothers ('geges') and big sisters ('jiejies'). William is pure joy."

17

The doctor who loved music

What you leave behind is not what is engraved in stone monuments, but what is woven into the lives of others.

PERICLES

In the autumn of 2004, with the palliative care unit taking in children with conditions classified as terminal, Robin and Joyce were trying to find help for children with some extreme medical needs and some very rare conditions. That October, Joyce was sent a little boy who had been abandoned and was not expected to live. Attached to his chest was a large, dark mass – a potential twin who had not developed. If the viable twin was to survive, then the mass needed to be removed.

Dr Yih at Beijing United Family Hospital carried out the difficult and risky procedure, and Cameron, the child, survived the surgery. He was still a very malnourished little boy afterwards and Joyce needed to continue his nursing at New Hope Foster Home, but after a few months the difference in Cameron was startling. He was sitting in his high chair at the Home, staring excitedly at his bowl of noodles, with his round, dark eyes wide open in his sweet face, as his nanny tested to see if his food was cool enough.

Joyce also received S, a baby with unclear gender and an open bladder. She arranged a chromosome test to understand how to proceed. The results came back that the baby was a boy, but he was going to need very specialist surgery to allow him a functioning bladder. However, Joyce knew someone who could give the baby the best possible chance in life. She turned on her computer and emailed Dr Ngan in Hong Kong.

* * *

In 2003 Dr John Ngan was working in Hong Kong as a children's urology surgeon. In his late forties, John looked much younger than his years, and his gentle manner meant that his young patients were always at ease and reassured when they met him. He was a successful surgeon and he and his young family enjoyed life in the vibrant Hong Kong Islands, but he was very disappointed that his unique area of specialization seemed to be going to waste.

John had trained extensively in extremely rare and complex cases in children's urology, becoming highly skilled at reconstructing open bladders – an unusual condition, called exstrophy, where the child is born with the bladder lying open like a small pancake on their tummy. The open bladder drips urine continuously and if not corrected early, the exposed bladder surface becomes scarred and eventually becomes irreparable. A bladder reconstruction is always a long and very specialized operation, needing a substantial recovery time of about six weeks. The surgeon must work alongside an orthopaedic surgeon, who will bring the splayed pelvic bones closer together so that the child can walk normally.

John had lived in the USA as a fellow of Seattle Children's Hospital, and it was here that he was mentored by world experts in particularly difficult open-bladder cases and, while still a young doctor, he became highly specialized in this very rare condition that affects only two babies in every million. But when the time came for Dr Ngan to return to his home in Hong Kong, the only doors that opened for him were in private clinics, and so he decided to take on a daily schedule of routine urinary infections and hernias in order to support his young family. Hong Kong simply did not have the population size to present many cases of bladder exstrophy.

He said to his wife, "I've had all this training and now I'm back in private practice and I'm just doing circumcisions all day. It doesn't make sense at all."

One of John's friends was involved with a Canadian medical mission called EMAS. John was invited to go out with them on a trip to China, but at that time EMAS did not have the needs or the facilities to put John's skills to use, so he returned home with no further plans to visit China.

Some months later, John got an email from a surgeon he had met during the EMAS medical trip to Suzhou in China. Could John possibly help a four-year-old boy who was living in a local CWI? The little boy, whose name was Jin-Jin, constantly leaked urine and had to wear diapers. In China, no child is allowed to attend school until they are dry, so the little boy had no chance of getting an education.

John asked the surgeon to send him a photo of the child's condition so he could get a better idea of what was wrong. In those days the computer took a while to download high-definition photos, but when John saw the picture slowly beginning to come through, he found himself bursting into tears. He was looking at a bladder exstrophy, the rare condition that he had been specifically trained to sort out. He thought, "OK, this is why I am here in Hong Kong. I can really help this child."

John obtained permission to carry out the operation in the

Hong Kong Matilda Hospital, where he worked. But even in the largest of hospitals with the most modern facilities, this was still going to be a very difficult case. John would also needed to find an orthopaedic children's surgeon to assist with the pelvic bone reconstruction needed to allow the child to walk properly, as well as an experienced children's anaesthetist. There was one further crucial detail: he was going to have to find the money to pay for a major operation, plus all the accompanying medical bills.

But when John explained to friends and colleagues what he was trying to do, he found that they all wanted to help. He was able to bring the little boy out to Hong Kong and with a team of doctors and surgeons, John carried out a successful operation to close Jin-Jin's bladder.

Jin-Jin made an excellent recovery. He was going to need some follow-up surgery, but John was delighted to hear from Jin-Jin's foster family that the little boy had started school and could not wait to go back there the next morning.

John found that once or twice a year he would get another email from China asking for help with a child. He decided to set up a small fund in Hong Kong called the Matilda Foundation, to help provide financially for the surgeries.

As China has a huge population, John was beginning to see that even for such a rare condition, it must add up to quite a lot of exstrophy cases. So one evening, while he was staying in Chicago for a conference, John was sitting beside a computer and decided to try typing "China" and "exstrophy" into an internet search.

The site for New Hope Foster Home popped up at the top of the list. He began to read through the information on the home and was stunned: this foster home was dealing with exstrophy cases, spina bifida, heart problems and many serious conditions that involved tertiary care in a major hospital. He decided to send Joyce an email.

John wrote, "It looks as if you might need some help. I live quite close by in Hong Kong. I have the right training to help with complicated bladder problems. If you need some help, I welcome questions."

The next day John opened his email inbox and found a long list of questions from Joyce. They were all about challenging problems, but John was able to reply to all her queries.

After the third or fourth exchange of emails, John wrote, "Hi Joyce, I can see that this is not something that we can sort out by email. I'm coming out to see what you have there."

So in 2005, John made his first trip out to New Hope Foster Home. He also took a friend along with him, Dr Yu, a neurosurgeon specializing in spina bifida. The neurosurgeon had travelled to Beijing thinking that he was just going on an information-gathering trip, with perhaps a bit of sightseeing on the side, but when Dr Yu examined one of the babies he realized that he was looking at an emergency case. The baby had a spinal bulge that was in danger of leaking out. Dr Yu said that he was willing to operate right away, and John offered to assist him.

John was still in contact with the hospital in Suzhou where he had helped Jin-Jin three years earlier. The staff and health minister there soon had the signed papers they needed to operate. John and his friend extended their leave, and travelled out to the hospital in Suzhou. Joyce sent the baby with two helpers on the overnight train and in the morning Dr Yu and Dr Ngan operated, and the baby came through with no complications.

John began visiting New Hope Foster Home on a regular basis to offer his skills in rare bladder conditions. He was also organizing hospital places in Hong Kong for some of Joyce's babies with other medical conditions. Over time John began to build up a network of surgeons in Hong Kong and China who were ready to step in and help with bladder surgeries. He and a group of other medical friends decided to raise funds for emergency surgeries. This initiative was called the China Orphan Outreach Foundation.

As well as being doctors, John and Dr Yu were also amateur violinists. Along with several other doctors who enjoyed performing classical music, in 2003 they had set up a foundation called MedArt. Its purpose was to take music to those people who are left out and forgotten in society – prisoners, psychiatric patients, and old people consigned to care homes.

They began to take their music to the bedsides of chronically sick patients. They played in prison cells, and in front of screaming psychiatric patients. It led to some strange situations. John and his friends found themselves jamming music with inmates in prison wings where almost everyone had killed somebody.

John explains: "We wanted to get to people that were in need, who were bored and who would never be able to go to a concert any more. But we wanted to do it mostly to show that people care. So it's a very interesting experience – to educate ourselves that these people are around us, remind ourselves that the only way to get them back into the community is to show that we accept them."

The China Orphan Outreach Foundation became a part of the MedArt Program and even organized a concert in Hong Kong where Lang Lang, the exuberant young concert pianist from China, gave a performance to help raise funds for the medical needs of orphans.

John and his wife also fostered a little girl from New Hope Foster Home. Two-year-old Lucy had arrived at the Home with eye cancer. Her condition seemed hopeless, and Joyce emailed a copy of Lucy's scan to Dr Yu, preparing herself to hear that she must treat Lucy palliatively. But Dr Yu replied: "Send Lucy out to Hong Kong immediately." They would find an eye specialist to help her.

Sadly, they were not able to save the eye that was most affected by cancer, but the cancer in the remaining eye went into remission and they began the long process of surgery, chemotherapy and laser treatment to save Lucy's sight. It was extremely expensive, but John and Joyce received funds to cover all the hospital bills, and Lucy began to respond well. She settled down and enjoyed beginning preschool. She also began to develop as a little person. John and his family found that she adored dancing to music, although, to John's amusement, it was only to classical music. She also became a great fan of the wrestling bouts on TV during the Beijing Olympics, enthusiastically cheering on China.

When Lucy returned to New Hope after two years of treatment, she continued to make a good recovery and is now a fit and active little girl. She has managed to keep her full head of hair and was given a very realistic prosthetic eye. Most people meeting Lucy for the first time now would notice only what a beautiful little girl she is.

Lucy was later matched with her own forever family, to the delight of John and his family. Joyce too was overjoyed at the news, profoundly grateful for all that John had done to help Lucy. She adds, "If not for Dr Yu and John, Lucy would not be alive today."

* * *

It was late in 2004 when the Hills took in S, the abandoned baby who appeared to have indeterminate sex organs as well as an open bladder – although in every other way he was healthy and not at all underweight. It must have seemed to the parents and the CWI that nothing could be done to help him, but Joyce made a call to Dr John Ngan in Hong Kong. After the baby's chromosomes were tested, and the results confirmed that they were in fact male, the baby, named S, was flown out to Hong Kong with his nanny to see Dr Ngan.

Many doctors could replace a child's bladder inside the body, but few could carry out such an operation without causing nerve damage and permanent incontinence. But John had the experience and specialist training to be able to not only rebuild a functioning bladder but also locate the baby's male organs internally and bring them out into the right place. S would need a couple more surgeries and a lot of careful nursing, but he made a full recovery from the reconstructions. He was a bright little baby, quick to learn and strong and energetic, and with decided opinions. He was soon happily settled with adoring foster parents in the village near to New Hope, and three years later he was adopted by his own forever family in the USA.

Dr Ngan continues to help many children at New Hope to lead a full life, and so have a better chance of being adopted one day, or sometimes to simply have the chance to live. He and many other specialist doctors from around the world are the quiet heroes who help Joyce make such a difference to children who were once abandoned without hope because they needed surgery.

John says that one of the dreams he has is that parents in far corners of China will hear about the work that he and Joyce and others do. "Then," says John, "they might be more hopeful and instead of abandoning the child, they might come along and get surgery done."

18

The opening of a second palliative care unit

It is not how much we do, but how much love we put in the doing. It is not how much we give, but how much love we put in the giving.

MOTHER TERESA

By March 2006, the Hills were caring for a total of forty-eight babies at New Hope Foster Home in Beijing, as well as twelve babies in the Jiaozuo special care unit some 600 miles south-west of Beijing.

In spite of the distances involved, the palliative care unit in South Henan was running well. As visitors entered the sixth-floor unit, the peach-coloured walls and bouncy Tigger murals announced a hopeful, loving standard of care. The issues about Joyce being allowed to run the unit on the same principles as New Hope were now resolved and a red velvet banner on the wall – a gift from the CWI – announced Dr Joyce Hill as director of the unit in large, gold lettering. The CWI director was so proud of the unit that he brought reporters and television crews around to see how well the children were being cared for.

The only shadow across the opening of the new unit was the

knowledge that the same needs existed in CWIs across a country of 1.3 billion people.

At the next Board meeting Rob and Joyce gave the team the good news: 40 per cent of the babies in the palliative unit had received the help they needed and had gone on to live.

"You can save that many lives for just $20,000!" said JT. "We should open more units."

Rob paused. He had further news. Director Pei from the CWI in Luoyang, who had once sent them the baby on the overnight train for an emergency stomach operation, had recently been to see the special care unit. His immediate question to Joyce and Rob was, "How soon can you open a unit like that here in Luoyang?"

This was a great opportunity; it was only possible to open a unit in a CWI by invitation, and they really needed to be on the ground in the CWI so that they could help the very sick babies as soon as they came in, in order to have the best chance of saving lives. Joyce was already seeing what a difference it made to the children, to be able to scoop them up and arrange treatment as soon as possible.

This second palliative and special care unit would be much larger, with 45 beds, since the CWI in Luoyang had at least 600 children. It was another 200 miles further out from Beijing than Jiaozuo. It would be a large project that involved travelling over 800 miles each way.

Rob had been regularly working on building projects now for five years, and although as an engineer he always enjoyed the challenges of construction projects, building in China always had its own problems. Someone who knew all about working with teams of local builders in China was Simon Wu, an interior designer from Hong Kong who was now based in Beijing. When large global companies began moving into China, Simon was able to produce the kind of elegant marble and glass showpieces wanted by the new Dior and Fendi stores in Beijing. Jing Littlewood was so impressed by the way that Simon had redesigned his own Beijing flat, with simple lines and elegant materials, that she asked him to help her with her own house renovation. After much persuasion, he agreed, and once he had worked his magic on Jing's house, he was asked by many of Jing's friends in Beijing to renovate their houses.

Jing and Toby took Simon out to New Hope to have lunch with Robin and Joyce, and to see if there was any possibility that he could help Rob with the refurbishment of the new palliative care unit in Luoyang.

Simon was not quite sure how his skills could fit in with such a project. His area of expertise was in refurbishments for the luxury shops serving the wealthiest people in Beijing. But as soon as he met the children and saw round New Hope, Simon realized that the Hills were doing something very special. The quiet and elegant man in a designer jacket stood holding a baby and looking very thoughtful. When Rob unrolled the plans for the fifth-floor-unit refurbishment in the CWI in Luoyang, Simon immediately volunteered his help.

On a cold day at the end of April, Joyce and Robin flew down to Luoyang with Simon, Toby and Jing to discuss plans for the new 45-bed unit. They met with the director and staff of the CWI and then looked around the series of empty bedrooms and corridors that would soon be the new palliative unit. They visited the rest of the home and left saddened but determined to press on with the refit as quickly as possible.

Simon was very impressed by all that Rob had done in China. More than anyone, he understood how hard it must have been for him as an expatriate to get so many building projects up and running. With his business connections throughout China, Simon knew how to source things locally and was able to ensure that the unit was fitted with durable materials without spending large amounts of money – no small feat when building materials are all sold from an enormous bazaar of local shops with every item needing to be bartered for.

The Hills soon realized that Simon approached working for the least privileged members of society, for no financial reward, just as professionally as his work for his usual glamorous and wealthy clients. Simon had fitted out some of the most exclusive shops in Beijing, but was now fitting out bathrooms and bedrooms for those children considered to be "the least of the least". It seemed to Rob that God was underlining a point.

Simon and his team rapidly transformed the fifth floor of the institution into a bright and cheerful outpost of New Hope Foster Home. Four weeks after the first internal windows were knocked through to let more light into the central corridors, the Hills were delighted to be able to show the CWI director around the fresh suite of rooms.

Joyce spent another month equipping the unit, and then Linda agreed to move from Beijing to live in the small flat in the unit and act as its on-site manager. Joyce was very proud of Linda. This shy and diffident lady, who had once so faithfully helped to love and care for Katie as her nanny, and had been there at the airport to welcome them home, had now blossomed into a dependable and capable manager. Joyce had no worries at all about leaving the daily management of the unit and its staff under her supervision.

In September 2006, Joyce and Linda took thirteen sick or premature babies into the Luoyang Special Care Unit and introduced them to their new nannies. Exactly three years earlier, Director Pei had sent them baby Zachary on the overnight train to see if the Hills could save him. Now they had a 45-bed unit in the CWI, to help other baby Zacharys straight away.

Director Pei, the Hills, the Littlewoods, Simon and Marsha stood in a row at the official opening ceremony and together snipped a red ribbon held up by a line of ladies in traditional red silk dresses. There were firecrackers, traditional dances and music from the children in the main CWI, and the director held a banquet in a local restaurant – since nothing can be done officially in China without a formal meal. But for Simon and all those who had helped to get the new unit in place, the best opening celebration was to see the children being so well cared for in their suite of new rooms.

Joyce wrote in the Christmas newsletter: "At the end of 2005, we cared for 60 children. Today, we are caring for 102 children in our units in 3 different cities. The rate of expansion has astounded us, but we are willing to serve exactly as directed by God."

Amber came home from Scotland to celebrate Christmas, and Ryan was also home after his first term in Australia, keen to check on his network of bike tracks through the fields behind the home. Aron (Joyce's eldest biological son) and his family flew in from Indiana. Joyce and Robin enjoyed a wonderful time together with family, appreciative that their children were so supportive of them staying on in China and not always being readily available due to the travel distances involved. The babies had a wild Christmas lunch with little red Santa hats and then lots of ripping of paper from gifts.

New Year brought a lion dance performed by the children and an excellent display of fireworks engineered by Rob and Ryan. The families and babies from the foster programme came and joined in the party, and Love Without Boundaries presented all the children with traditional red silk suits, warmly padded for winter, that made the babies look even more adorable than they usually did.

It was amazing to see how much had happened over the previous few years and how much the work had grown, but if the Hills could have looked forward into the next year, they might have been surprised to learn just how quickly they were going to once again double the number of children in their care.

One thing the Hills did know, however, was that they could not help the children on their own. They were continually grateful for the many people who supported the babies, each act of kindness contributing to the patchwork quilt of help that would change the lives of many children, one child at a time.

19

Amy Eldridge and Love Without Boundaries

Every child counts.

As Joyce and Robin began to help an increasing number of children, they began to meet other people trying to make a difference to the lives of needy orphans. Two friendships were to prove especially significant as the years went by.

In 2004 the Hills got to know Amy Eldridge of Love Without Boundaries, and with her support opened a medical unit inside New Hope to give specialist barrier nursing to children in need of pre- and post-operative care.

Amy, an American housewife from Oklahoma, first visited China in 2003. She is young, blonde and smartly dressed. If you met her briefly, and said hello to this cheerful and chatty lady, you might assume that she was just like any other busy middle-class mum. But Amy is passionate about helping needy children. As well as doing the school run and the weekly shop for her family, she can be found organizing nutritional, medical and educational programmes for orphans in provinces all across China.

Amy's involvement with China started when she travelled to

Guangzhou to adopt the first of her two Chinese daughters. Her daughter came from a CWI in Shantou, but all adoptions to the USA and Europe take place in Guangzhou town, and so parents usually go to the now famous White Swan Hotel to collect their son or daughter. On the day that Amy went to the hotel and her daughter Anna was placed in her arms, something strange happened.

"I heard God speak to me," says Amy. "He said, 'I want you to go to Shantou.'"

Amy had already been told that this was officially not possible, so she flew home. It took three years to find out any information about Anna's CWI in Shantou, but finally Amy was able to fly back to see where Anna had started her life. She says, "The orphanage I walked into could not be further from the bright, clean orphanage that is Shantou today… it was one of the saddest days of my life."

While she was visiting Anna's CWI, she came across a little boy named Kang. Amy says, "He was dying of heart disease, as he had four holes in his heart. The orphanage told me that there were no funds for surgery. My own heart broke in two that day, and half stayed in China forever. As I watched him struggle for breath, I felt completely helpless."

Amy left some "milk money" with the CWI and went back home. What else could she do? She was just an ordinary mum.

At 2 a.m. in the morning, a week after she got back home, Amy heard God speak again. She says, "It was loud enough to wake me up and it was very specific: 'Get out of bed and help that child.'"

She pushed back the warm covers and went upstairs to her computer. She typed in the words, "baby hearts".

Amy says: "That began it. Of course, Shantou sent me the files for four children and not just for Kang… and I felt this immense pressure that I had to heal them all. And thankfully God showed me so clearly that it *wasn't* me that had to heal them… that with His help we could pull people together to save lives. I told God on my knees that I was willing to do anything He asked of me. And that week $60,000 came into my mailbox for those children, and they were healed."

The surgery for all four babies was successful. But then Amy got a call from the hospital in China. Baby Kang had gone into kidney failure and his CWI had no means of getting the kind of medical equipment a baby needed for kidney dialysis. Amy went straight into action and arranged for specialist equipment to be brought in, but after a couple of days Dr Li called to say it wasn't working. They needed to let the baby go.

Amy sat in the park near her kids' school, sobbing. When she got back home, she sent out a final prayer request for baby Kang, "asking that it be passed out on the internet, for everyone to pray that this child would feel our love as he died from this world. I got hundreds and hundreds of emails from strangers that they were praying for Kang. And the next day… he rallied. I can't say just how much it means to me when his mother, Anne, sends pictures from Sweden. He is a perfectly healthy and happy little boy. He is so beautiful, and he is a miracle child to me."

In 2003, Amy and a group of other adoptive parents came together to register a charity in Oklahoma called "Love Without Boundaries", with three words as their guiding principle: "Every child counts".

A few months later, Amy and three other ladies travelled back to China and visited CWIs not normally seen by Westerners. They took formula, clothes and toys. Though devastated by what she saw, Amy says she felt very positive about trying to help out, humming hymns to herself to keep her spirits up. But one day, the total of all the needs there suddenly overwhelmed her. She came to a complete standstill on the CWI steps, physically and emotionally crushed to the point that she felt like she might black out.

The hymns stopped; just a bleak silence. Amy says, "We all came back from that trip changed people. And we all tried to deal with it in our own ways. I stopped going to church… I couldn't face anyone who would come up with a smile and nonchalantly say, 'How was China?'

"One Sunday, when I couldn't face walking into church again, I dropped my kids at Sunday school and drove out into the country and just started arguing and yelling at God. I was crying and I said, 'Don't these kids mean anything to You? How can You allow that to happen?' I really poured it out.

"And then I had such a feeling of love and peace come over me when God said, 'I am their DADDY, and every child is important to Me.' Over the next half hour I realized that God was calling me to China long-term… He had taken me there for a reason and opened doors that few foreigners got to enter. And so I turned my whole life over that day to God. I promised Him that so long as it was His will, I would be His hands and feet in China."

A few days later, a woman knocked on Amy's door. She attended Amy's church, but they didn't know each other very well. "This might sound really strange," the woman told Amy, "but I need to give you a message. I have no idea what this means, but God wants you to know that He heard you on Sunday morning, and He accepts."

Love Without Boundaries grew very fast to encompass a worldwide base of seventy volunteers, delivering extensive programmes to provide essential food, medical help and education for needy orphans across many provinces in China.

Like Joyce, Amy became increasingly aware that many babies had medically treatable conditions such as heart, palate and bowel problems, but they needed surgery if they were going to survive. Soon, Love Without Boundaries was sending forty parentless children a month for surgical help. But there were often many issues that the children had to contend with before and after surgery.

On one of her trips Amy heard from a rural CWI about a baby who could not eat. He had a cleft palate and they could not get the specialist bottles needed to feed him, and so they asked Amy if she could help. LWB had a team of cleft-palate surgeons from the USA who were about to do a series of surgeries in Luoyang, so Amy replied that if they could get the baby there, he could have surgery. Within thirty minutes, the CWI staff had the baby bundled up and on his way in a car.

Six hours later the nannies hurried into the hospital, holding the baby. Amy could see immediately that the child was tiny for his age, and too underweight to cope with any surgery.

The team took the little boy, bathed him, put him in clean clothes and then fetched a cleft bottle. Amy says they have never been able to figure out why such bottles are not available in China. They filled it up with warm formula and the baby had the first full bottle of his life. They named him Hercules because he held on so tightly when he was being fed, so keen was he to take a full feed. "I don't think any of us had a dry eye when he finished," says Amy.

Hercules continued to take bottles through the night, and by the next day looked much better. But he was still nowhere near the weight needed to undergo surgery. The CWI aunties were very disappointed. Amy sent them off with a bag of formula and specialist bottles, and promised to make sure that as soon as he reached 10 pounds in weight, Hercules would have surgery. But it was hard to watch the baby leave without getting the surgery he needed, and the team cried to see him go.

After she got back home, Amy could not forget Hercules and felt she should go back to China and see him at his CWI. It was their china (twentieth) wedding anniversary, so Amy's husband gave her a ticket to fly out to China and see Hercules as an anniversary gift.

Baby Hercules was hungrily sucking on his two fingers and getting weaker and weaker. As Amy held him, she could feel that he was getting too tired to keep fighting. The nannies were doing their best, but there were so many babies and not enough hands for a slow feeder like Hercules.

"He really needs one-to-one care," the nannies told Amy.

Amy knew where Hercules needed to go if he was to have a chance. The Hills had helped Amy with medically critical children before, but she also knew that they always had a long waiting list. She took a deep breath and called Joyce.

"There's this baby…" Amy began.

"How fast can you get him here?" Joyce answered.

As she hung up the phone, Amy knew that Hercules was going to make it.

When Amy, the CWI nannies and the other LWB helpers drove to the airport to take Hercules to Beijing, a blizzard came down and they had a couple of near misses in the traffic. When they got to the airport, they found it filled with stranded and upset people. Yet even though they could not feel their toes any more, Amy and the others sat in the airport smiling and laughing, happy to know that Hercules would soon be on his way to getting better. People came up to them in the chilly waiting room and said, "You're having too much fun. Let us know your secret."

All flights out were cancelled that day, and the trains were booked up for New Year, but somehow Amy managed to find spaces and got Hercules and two aunties onto a train to Beijing, where Joyce would have someone waiting to take him home.

Hercules soon had his own nannies at New Hope and was starting to gain weight. It is always moving to see the change in a baby once they can get enough to eat. Gaunt children who arrive looking old and emaciated begin to look like babies a month later – bonny, alert and well fed. At one point Amber suggested that New Hope be called "The Fat Baby Farm".

Amy keeps a photo of Hercules on her office wall, along with all the other pictures of children who have come through against the odds. She says, "Late at night, I will take a moment to look at each one of them and say a prayer of thanksgiving that they are still alive."

LWB carries out an average of forty life-saving surgeries every month, but post-operative care can be problematic for the children. Amy realized that at New Hope, Joyce was able to offer standards of care that meant heart- or cleft-surgery babies could have the chance to make a full recovery. So in 2006, she provided funding through LWB to help Joyce open a nine-bed pre- and post-surgery ward within the New Hope building. It was rapidly increased in size to take eighteen children. The new Heartbridge unit was placed across the hallway from the main office upstairs. A large bottle of hand sanitizer and a notice outside the unit door reminded everyone that this area had children with compromised immunity who needed barrier nursing. Love Without Boundaries also provided funds to help build the extension where the unit is housed as well as to equip and run the unit.

If friendship is based on shared interests, then it is no surprise that Joyce and Amy have become such firm friends. They are able to understand and support each other in what it means to try and save the life of just one more baby, with all the accompanying strains and heartaches. Amy and Joyce also enjoy swapping emails about their large families of children growing into their independent phase, discussing when to step in with help and when to let children make their own mistakes as they move into the adult world.

Love Without Boundaries also supports 300 children in fifteen cities throughout China in foster-care programmes where babies are able to have more individual care and better outcomes than in many large institutions.

As soon as New Hope began to have children who were healed and healthy, Robin and Joyce started to keep an ear to the ground for suitable families in the villages who might like to care for a child in their own home as foster parents. This would give the children the chance to experience family life, and also free up a bed for a new child needing medical help. Joyce was clear that the standards in the village foster homes had to match those that were provided in the main foster home. She says, "We are very selective when assessing homes and families for our children and once a child is placed with a family, the home staff make scheduled and unscheduled visits to make sure that the childcare is up to standard."

Many of the couples who volunteered were older parents who had seen their only child begin school or leave for college. They were now very happy to have a toddler to care for again. There were soon twenty children living with families in the rural community around the home, all enjoying family life and beautifully cared for by their foster parents.

The Hills were thrilled when Amy offered to help sponsor

the foster programme at Hope. Amy was impressed by the high adoption rate and the excellent care given the babies. She arranged for a LWB volunteer to visit regularly and keep in touch with the babies' needs.

Rose, a trainee Filipina nurse who was working in the preschool, helped Joyce administer the foster programme. Rose had fluent Chinese and a gift for putting local people at ease, and was a huge favourite with the nannies in the home. She made regular visits to the foster families to see how they were getting on.

On a warm summer's day, Rose drove out to see the parents of Spencer, a little boy who was now well enough to be adopted. Spencer had received complicated surgery in Hong Kong, and though generally well, he had needed to return for follow up surgery over three years. He had come through some unusually tricky and delicate bladder surgery very successfully, thanks to Dr Ngan.

Spencer was a high energy, confident little boy, very well cared for by his adoring foster parents. Rose was going to take some photos of Spencer and his Chinese foster family for his memory scrapbook. With the volunteers' help, Rose compiled the personal folders of pictures, paintings and memories that were given to each adoptive family to help them share something of the child's time at New Hope – and give the child a reminder of where they first grew up and who their nannies were.

It was early afternoon and the driver took the road through Beiwu – a crossroads of one-storey shops covered in dusty white tiles. As always in summer, there were items of washing drying on coat hangers in the trees, and people sitting out on folding chairs in the afternoon sun, to play Mahjong or chat while little dogs ran around their legs. The Chinese barbecue where the volunteers liked to eat sometimes in the evening was just beginning to open up its smoke-blackened windows. Soon the lines of fairy lights would be switched on and the scuffed picnic chairs and tables set out on the pavement.

The car turned off down a narrow side road, through an ornamental gate that announced entry into a village community. Here, everything was well swept and extremely tidy. Every rural village is painted in its own communal colour; this one was painted dark pink, with turquoise bands and insets of pretty Chinese paintings. The houses were one-storey cottages, all with roofs that sloped up at the corners to stop the good luck from draining away back into the earth. There were no windows facing onto the street; the narrow, walled roads had the closed-off, private feel that outsiders are generally presented with in the architecture of Chinese villages.

The car pulled up at the gates of a corner house, with its high-walled garden. A traditional ghost wall – placed there to stop ghosts, since they can only travel in straight lines – blocked the gate. Rose knocked and called several times, but gave up on etiquette and went in.

Inside, was the secret household life: a well-swept courtyard with a manicured vegetable garden and teepees of beans and tomatoes. Nearby a rack of washing was drying in the sun. The house was one room deep and spread around three sides of the garden, with large veranda-like windows opening onto the courtyard.

Spencer's foster parents appeared and greeted Rose warmly. They were an older couple but energetic and with smiles that made their eyes fold up into laughter lines. The foster father took evident pride in raising a foster son, although Rose knew that both he and his wife were equally doting parents when they had cared for their two foster daughters before Spencer.

Spencer's bedroom was a cool, white haven against the heat, with a floating white cloth to mark off the bathroom door. There was a TV and an imported Brio train – an exorbitantly expensive item, but the foster father has difficulty not spoiling Spencer.

On the wall was a framed montage of photos of Spencer over the past three years. He had arrived as a baby, and they now dreaded his departure – even though they were happy that he would soon have a forever family. The foster father got out photos of Spencer's new parent's in Texas, along with his seven new brothers and sisters. He explained to Rose that when he heard that it was such a big family, he was very upset and thought that Spencer would not get enough care. But having now met the family who came out to China and visited them, he feels that Spencer will be well looked after. And seeing the picture of the family in their garden in America, already with two adopted Chinese children, all looking happy and relaxed together, Rose agreed that she thought Spencer would indeed be happy. Nevertheless, it wasn't hard to see that sharing and mixing in with several siblings might take some getting used to for Spencer, who had so far been a doted-on, single child.

Mum also brought out photos of their two previous foster daughters, now settled with forever families in America. Rose put an arm around her when mum started to cry. They had been a very loving family for all their children, and had recently come to the decision that once Spencer left them they would not be able to go through the pain of another separation, but would give more time to their grown-up daughter and only grandchild.

Rose suggested taking a photo in the garden for Spencer's memory book. Mum went to change into her smart trousers, and they managed to get Spencer to stand still and stop working the camera – a very bright little four-year-old, he had already figured how to work it. Rose managed to get a great snapshot of the family in front of their crops.

Mum picked a large bag of tomatoes and cucumbers for Rose to take back to the nannies. They all came out to say goodbye at the gates, and a flock of birds settling on bunches of electricity wires overhead. A cyclist going past called out hello to the family and rang his bell, kept looking as he rode on past.

The foster parents and nannies in the villages around the home were all part of their local communities, where there was now great support for the way that the Hills were helping children who would not otherwise have had a chance to live a full life, or even survive. It was unusual to see children with handicaps in local communities, but here people had seen the children cared for, healed and thriving. The villagers said that the Hills must really love children.

20

Meeting the Chapman family

*God is right where He said He would be, among the poor,
the needy, the least. "So what now – now that you've
found Me?"*

STEVEN CURTIS CHAPMAN

The second friendship that was to prove very significant was
that of the Chapman family, who came from Nashville,
Tennessee.

One afternoon, a man in his early forties wearing a baseball
cap, T-shirt and grubby jeans turned up at New Hope asking if he
could visit the home. Some friends, he explained, had told him
that he really should come and see what Joyce and Robin were
doing.

Robin gave him the usual tour, and though Robin or Joyce may
have given it many times before, it is always a moving experience
for a new visitor to hear the details of what some of the children
have been through, and to see the difference between the pictures
of emaciated newborns, and the healthy toddlers waving from
their playroom windows. The man listened quietly and attentively,
but when they came to the well-organized storeroom, with its

rows of neatly stacked shelves and its rack of baby clothes hung up in descending size, a look of recognition came into his eyes.

"Mary Beth'll just love this!" he exclaimed.

He told the Hills that he and his wife had six children, and one of the things that made their life run smoothly was the fact that his wife loved to be really organized. He also told the Hills how his three youngest children, all daughters, were adopted from China.

By now, the Hills realized that they had seen Steven before, as the main musician performing songs at a fund-raiser concert in Beijing. He explained that his friends David Trask and Scott Hasenbalg, who had already been round to visit the home, worked with him as his road manager and project director; they were the ones who had insisted that he had to go and see New Hope Foster Home for himself.

As they carried on talking, the Hills found out that Steven was involved in supporting many adoptive families in the USA through a foundation he had set up called Show Hope. It became increasingly apparent to the Hills that this was someone who had the same heart to care for orphans. As they stood in the hallway saying goodbye, Steven asked if he could perhaps come back the following summer and bring his wife, Mary Beth, to see that storeroom for herself. And perhaps they could stay for a few days?

"Of course," Joyce told him.

When they went to church the next Sunday and mentioned Steven's visit to some of their American friends, Robin and Joyce began to realize just how widely known Steven was in the USA and how much his songs meant to a great many people. They headed out at the first opportunity to get hold of some of Steven's music and found out that they were already familiar with a lot of it and that some of Rob's favourite songs had in fact been written by Steven.

Steven Curtis Chapman had a long and distinguished career in American gospel music. He and Mary Beth had started out in the eighties as a penniless young couple, hoping that Steven could support them with a modest music career, and immediately they lost the few possessions they had in a house fire. But over the years, as Steven's songs connected with people, he sold over 10 million albums, with ten of his albums going gold and platinum. Steven ended up collecting a total of five Grammy awards and many other awards. The cheerful and unassuming man in a baseball cap and slightly scruffy jeans who visited the foster home that day had, however, mentioned none of these achievements.

Rob and Joyce also began to find out more about the orphan aid work that Steven and Mary Beth had started through their Show Hope Foundation to support orphans and aid adoption. Show Hope's first aim was always to unite orphans with their own family, and only if that was completely impossible would the foundation then do all it could to support adoptions, helping many families each year cover the fees that would otherwise prevent them from adopting.

The Show Hope Foundation also supported some of the many, many children who would never get adopted, who were destined to live out their lives in orphanages of very limited means in places such as Uganda, El Salvador, Romania and Russia.

Steven and Mary Beth began the Show Hope Foundation after they brought their first adopted daughter, Shaohannah Hope, home from China in 2000. As they stepped out of the plane with baby Shaoey warmly wrapped up against the March winds, they were astonished to find Nashville Airport crowded with hundreds of people waiting to welcome them home – this was just before security regulations prevented people from meeting people at the flight gate. The gate area was packed with friends, family and even newspaper reporters. It was evident that Shaoey's adoption had touched a lot of folk.

As they walked to the car, people came up and shared that they would love to adopt one day but they just couldn't afford the adoption fees.

Mary Beth's reply was immediate: "Well, call me next week. Let me get over jet lag and we'll figure out a way to help you."

So Mary Beth committed herself to helping a family here and there with some of the adoption fees as the needs came up, but it soon became clear that the issue was far bigger than any personal resources. So, in 2003, Mary Beth and Steven set up the Show Hope Foundation, and began to fund-raise in a serious way. Steven held benefit concerts, and each year they managed to double the number of families they could help.

* * *

The Chapman family's journey to adopting Shaoey started some three years earlier, triggered by a passionate but rather small adoption advocate – their eleven-year-old daughter Emily. In 1997 Mary Beth took Emily with her on a trip with Compassion Aid and they were able to visit a child they were sponsoring in an orphanage in Haiti. Emily was deeply affected by meeting the children and came up with an idea to help: why didn't her parents adopt one of the children?

Mary Beth explained why this was not practical, but Emily was not giving up. She bought books on international adoption, left her parents notes on their pillows with facts and figures, and got her brothers Will and Caleb to sign a petition.

Finally, Mary Beth decided that this had to stop after Emily made a huge fuss one evening, complaining because Mary Beth was going to watch the boys' baseball game instead of going to an adoption conference where Steven was due to sing.

She sat Emily down. "Look," she said. "If you bring back every pamphlet you can find at this conference, I promise I will read them all. But after that, this has to end. No more."

Emily agreed.

So the next day Mary Beth started to read through the mound of pamphlets. But instead of racing through them and handing them back to Emily, she found that she wanted to read on. Over the next few days, she also found that she was noticing things in a new light as she read through her Bible studies.

When Mary Beth told Steven that she wanted to adopt, he told her that he had come to the same conclusion. Together, they went and broke the news to Emily and the boys.

So after negotiating the adoption maze as complete novices, in March 2000 the Chapman family found themselves sitting together in a hotel room in China waiting to meet Shaoey for the first time. Mary Beth admits that she was a very scared mother of three just then, but the moment she held the tiny bundle, her new daughter, in her arms, something happened.

"I finally got it," Mary Beth says. "God was right there, whispering, *This is how I view you. You were an orphan and I adopted you into my family.*"

The Chapmans went home to Nashville feeling a very complete family. Steven says, "For us, this was a one-time deal. I was sure of that. Really sure."

But two years later, while they were attending the dedication ceremony of their friend's newly adopted daughter – the ninth child in the Coley family of four biological and five adopted children – it seemed to Steven that God was saying, "It's messy and uncomfortable, and I know you have concerns and fears, but if you trust me with these things, I'm inviting you into this adventure again."

A year later, the adoption date for Steveny Joy came through.

With their busy lives and five growing children, life in the Chapmans' house was now exhausting, rewarding and extremely "complete". Or so they thought.

In 2004, Steven was back in China and while in Beijing he met an American couple who were taking care of a baby in their foster home. Maria had once been ill and abandoned, but now she was getting better. The couple hoped that she might one day be adopted by a family. Steven held baby Maria and chatted to her, and felt profoundly affected.

That night Steven phoned back home in tears, and told Mary Beth about Maria.

"Don't even think about it!" Mary Beth told him.

But by the time Steven got back to Nashville, he found Mary Beth had all the adoption papers ready, spread out on the desk.

"I think we're supposed to go and get Maria," she told him.

* * *

Mary Beth found herself totally in love once more, with this little girl with such a huge grin and love of joining in with all the family. "Imagine my surprise," she says, "when, not once, not twice, but three times, these little treasures captured my heart."

Mary Beth also learned that there were some things that were special to being adopted. She says, "Adopted children, in my opinion, have little holes in their hearts. They carry with them a bit of sadness that they don't even identify with... yet." She felt that for even the most loving parents there was only so far one could completely heal that hole. She felt that it was only by helping the girls to understand how much they were also loved by God that she could help them heal that hurt completely.

By the end of 2004, the Show Hope Foundation was not only assisting a considerable number of adoptions, but also supporting a wide range of orphan aid projects across the world. After the Chapman family's third adoption Steven and Mary Beth began to search for ways to help children with needs in China.

Steven did a range of concert tours in Asia and says that he was able to meet many wonderful people working in China, but did not get any clear match to the kind of work he and Mary Beth wanted to do. Then in 2005, Steven walked into Joyce's storeroom at New Hope, and something went "click".

The following summer, Steven and Mary Beth paid their first visit to the Hills and met some of the children. They were able to return a year later, in 2006, bringing with them their six children, plus David and Scott and several other friends.

Much had changed in the foster home in the year since they first visited. Zachary had gone to live with his own mother and his buddy Toby Isaiah had received hand surgery and was now on his CWI's list to go forward for adoption.

Steven and Mary Beth were also able to meet some of the new children who had recently come to New Hope from the then newly opened special care unit in the CWI in Jiaozuo, including Rebekah – the baby who had first alerted the Hills to the needs there and who had once been given up to die. Rebekah was now running round the home in Beijing, a very cute and very alive, sturdy little toddler.

That summer the Hills had just received the go-ahead to open their second palliative care unit, in the Luoyang CWI. Mary Beth and Emily asked if they could fly down with Joyce to find out more about the planned unit.

They visited the babies. It was a devastating day. As they walked through the CWI's bleak fifth floor, the renovations and new beds still only plans, it was not easy to see where the Hills were going to begin. The needs were huge and the Hills had taken on a large and difficult project. Mary Beth and Steven decided that they wanted to do whatever they could to help the Hills reach these very sick babies, and they went home to the USA committed to finding ways to support them.

By their next visit, a year later, Mary Beth and Steven were able to return to Luoyang with Joyce and visit the newly opened palliative care unit there. The fifth floor of the CWI now looked like a wing of the home back in Beijing. Little boys with cerebral palsy were scooting around a playroom in special walkers, while cheerful Chinese nursery rhymes played and nannies arrived with their bowls of noodles ready for lunch. At the end of the corridor, other nannies cradled some very small and thin babies. These children were too frail and sick to endure any further treatment, but were being held and loved as they were allowed to die in peace and with pain relief.

Any baby whose condition was medically treatable had already been moved on to the Hills' foster home in Beijing and were now either receiving the surgery and help they needed, or were being built up to cope with it.

As they walked round the new Special Care Unit, Rob explained that an opportunity to help even more children had already come up. Rob and Joyce had got to know Director Pei very well. He was a man in late middle age, with a wise and somewhat sad expression, always seeking to do the best he could for the children. The children were his priority, even if his resources could not meet all he would like to do, and he had also grown to respect and trust the Hills.

He had come to Rob with a new suggestion. The buildings of his Luoyang CWI were going to be rebuilt as part of a "Blue Skies" government initiative to improve the lives of children in CWIs. Director Pei offered the Hills a plot of land alongside the new CWI so that they could erect their own purpose-built home with much larger special-care facilities.

It was a huge opportunity to reach more of the neediest children. It was also a dauntingly big project, but the Hills had drawn up plans to construct a four-storey building on the same model as the home in Shunyi, Beijing.

When the Hills and the Chapmans were all back in the home in Beijing, eating supper and listening to music as they chatted around the table, Steven and Mary Beth surprised the Hills with a suggestion. They offered to finance all the building costs of the new home in Luoyang through the Show Hope Foundation and to commit to raise enough funds to meet the running costs – if Robin and Joyce would continue to run and manage it. Steven and Mary Beth explained that they simply wanted to help the Hills take their excellent standard of care to more children.

Ever since the day Mary Beth and Steven had walked out of the CWI where Shaoey had spent the first year of her life, aware of the large numbers of babies left lying there who would never find a family of their own, they had dreamed about building a home for those unwanted children. "Just looking at all these faces, you realize there's never going to be enough families," Mary Beth says.

But China was a very different culture. Over time they realized that they needed to partner with people already on the ground, who were culturally familiar with China and able to establish genuine and respectful relationships with local people, from nannies and cooks to officials and CWI directors – people like Robin and Joyce.

"We were really looking to partner with someone, or help someone here on the ground in China and then we just really connected heart-wise with Robin and Joyce. The first time we came out here, we stayed for a few days with them and just immediately fell in love with the children and the way things were being done – to see sick children being cared for at the level she cares for those children. We've been coming back each summer, spending longer each time. This is our home from home."

Rob and Joyce were stunned: the Chapmans' offer to support the new home in Luoyang was so generous and so all-encompassing that it was hard to take in. Later, Robin wondered if he had misheard, and so politely checked that they really wanted to go ahead with such a high level of support. The Chapmans came back with a very certain "yes".

Robin and Joyce had started to plan the new four-storey home in Luoyang without really knowing how they would provide for all the costs. But they had also gone forward with a firm belief that if that was what God wanted to do, then He would provide for it – and if they didn't get the funds to proceed, well then, it couldn't have been what God wanted. Now, in the space of a moment, they were being offered enough support to build and run the new home.

As Rob rolled out the architect's plans, they gathered round to look at them after supper that night. Mary Beth said, "Why a four-storey building? Why not make it six floors?"

The new home in Luoyang became a six-floor, 128-bed building: to save the lives of as many children as possible and give them a chance of being adopted one day by their own family, and to love, comfort and care for those children who would be too sick to save.

Steven and Mary Beth invited Rob and Joyce to speak at

the Show Hope conference in Nashville that autumn. Rob was amused by what seemed to be God's sense of humour when he found himself asked to speak on financial planning. Rob had always been and remained a very strong advocate of good financial planning, and considered that it was essential to be responsible about finance. However, the reality of what had happened since opening the first home in 2000 was that as they were catapulted into new opportunities to help children, and as they doubled the number of children they helped each year, so the Hills continually doubled their financial costs and commitments. This was not at all the kind of financial strategy Rob approved of. And yet, as he and Joyce accepted each call to help more and more children, things seemed to work out.

Rob had come to the conclusion that the most important aspect of financial planning was to be obedient to what God wanted to do. Time and time again, Rob and Joyce were taken back to that initial moment when they had decided to step into a new way of life. The image that remained with them was of standing on the edge of a great and powerful river, a river carrying God's love and provision. The most vital aspect in financial planning was not to stand on the banks with a collecting tin and good intentions, but to get into the river of what God really wanted to do, to bring His love to the marginalized and disregarded.

Once they were back in Nashville, the Chapmans threw themselves into raising funds for the new home with great energy and commitment. As work began on the new building, they and their executive director for Show Hope, Scott Hasenbalg, flew out to Luoyang with Rob and Joyce to see how it was progressing. The weather was cold but the team was excited to see how the building was starting to rise up storey by storey, out of the sea of mud and building debris.

Any passing local people might have been surprised to see five Westerners in hard hats all huddled with their arms around each other and their eyes shut in the middle of the building site, while bemused workmen wheeled barrows of concrete up ramps and swung buckets of bricks up bamboo scaffolding.

Mary Beth and Steven went back home greatly looking forward to seeing the building almost completed by their next visit in the summer. But the following year was to prove the most difficult time that their family had ever known.

21

The new home in Luoyang

*I have held many things in my hands, and I have lost
them all: but whatever I have placed in God's hands, that
I still possess.*

CORRIE TEN BOOM

At the end of 2007, the entire Hill clan gathered for the wedding of Amber to Marcio Batista in Scotland, where Amber was starting training as a doctor and Marcio was working for YWAM as a youth pastor. All the men of the family donned kilts and everyone joined in Scottish dances at a ceilidh party – they even sampled haggis. Aron, Joyce's eldest biological son, had some news for Joyce. He was now married with a little girl, but he had decided to make a career change and had won a scholarship to go back to college and train as a doctor. The family made plans for as many of them as possible to meet up again in China for the grand opening of the new home in Luoyang in a year's time.

Rob was kept extremely busy all that year supervising the new build in Luoyang and the considerable distances involved did not make the task any easier. The flight from Beijing to Luoyang takes one and a half hours, and as you travel south across mountain ranges and an endless expanse of fields in various tones of green, you get some idea of just how huge China is. Every so often, marooned in the green sea, there is a cluster of white with roads visible as neat lines, hinting at the orderly village communes.

A hundred million people live in Henan, one of the most populous provinces in China. It is also one of the poorest of China's regions, particularly in areas where people live in isolated forest villages.

Luoyang is Henan's second largest city, a sprawling and busy town with a slightly dishevelled and temporary feel. Smart new hotels for businessmen and tourists visiting the nearby Shaolin monks' temple stand cheek by jowl next to ramshackle old apartment blocks with rows and rows of grubby air-conditioner boxes jutting out, and windows festooned with washing. The air has a definite pall of grey pollution above the traffic, though there are still hundreds of bicycles waiting at the traffic lights in the wide, tree-lined roads – something no longer seen in Beijing, where taxis and Mercedes now fill the freeways and flyovers. Three-wheeled bike-carts sedately pull out and slow down the Luoyang cars, or leisurely road sweepers work in the middle of the road with enormous rag brooms, unconcerned as cars swerve around them.

But Luoyang is keen to catch up. New businesses and factories are fast turning it into an important economic centre. In the summer, the city roads are planted out with miles and miles of pink flowers along the central reservations as a statement of civic pride.

Warm, summer evenings see families out for a stroll round the brand-new shopping mall. Trees twinkle with blue fairy lights as hawkers spread out their blankets of jewellery or mobile-phone covers, or large promotional stands with teams of dancers and singers sell expensive medical services or promote state-of-the-art gym equipment, pop music pumping in the background.

In small courtyards in nearby apartment blocks, you can still hear, in the late-summer darkness, the sound of traditional Chinese music as the elderly residents practise Tai Chi to keep their limbs supple, in slow and elegant movements of sequential balancing.

Meanwhile down in the station terminal, migrant workers spread newspapers on the floor to sleep, or pale and exhausted young couples sleep on tatty bundles made up of their entire possessions, as they wait for the night train.

In the morning, as the day-staff and nannies arrive for work at the CWI, they might find that during the night someone has left by the gates a sports bag that sometimes moves a little, or simply a small bundle of blankets.

During his visits to the building site, Rob found some surprising interpretations of the building plans. On one visit, the main shell of the building finished, Director Pei took Rob up to the top to see the newly completed roof area. In the middle stood a brick structure that housed the elevator workings. It was not very remarkable, except that the director had had it painted it sky blue, with fluffy white clouds stencilled on top. The director asked Rob if he approved, and Rob agreed that yes, it was quite nice. It was certainly going to stand out like a beacon across the wide, flat countryside, Rob thought to himself.

Imagine Rob's surprise when some time later he got a telephone call to let him know that the entire six-storey building had since been painted sky blue with fluffy white clouds sprayed over it. Rob says that it was quite a good thing that there were 900 kilometres, Marsha as translator, and a telephone wire between him and the director when he found out.

Working with the local builders could be very frustrating – like trying to hit a moving target, Rob says. And yet somehow things got done, and done well. He says, "I think it happens by the grace of God that these places end up looking like they look, and that they work."

Even so, with such a large building project, it was a taxing process to try and keep to projected schedules, and the tentative opening date of autumn 2008 crept forward to the early summer of 2009.

* * *

In Nashville, the Chapmans were looking forward to returning to China the following summer. In the meantime, Steven and Mary Beth were delighted when Emily announced her engagement to Tanner, and the family held a party to celebrate.

Two days later Mary Beth was in the house, preparing a second family party to celebrate Caleb's graduation, when she heard some commotion out on the driveway.

She ran outside to see what was happening. Maria had been accidentally struck by a car in front of the house. The little girl was urgently airlifted to Nashville Vanderbilt Hospital for emergency treatment. Steven and Mary Beth drove to the hospital as fast as possible and Steven ran in to pray over Maria.

But as he made his way to Maria's room, the doctor stopped him and said that she had already died.

After Maria passed away, messages of consolation poured in from around the world, and the church in America got behind the family to pray and care for them. Thousands of people came to Maria's memorial service, and many more thousands shared the recording of her funeral ceremony on the internet. Maria had once been a child discarded on the street, given up as being too sick to live. Now the world understood that Maria was an irreplaceable treasure and a beloved daughter. Her loss was truly mourned across the world.

Robin and Joyce understood the pain of losing a child, after the sudden death of Natasha as a young woman, and as soon as they heard about Maria they arranged to fly out to Nashville to be with Steven and Mary Beth and support them at Maria's memorial service.

People were asked, rather than sending in flowers to the family, to donate to the Show Hope orphan fund. In the days and months that followed, Scott directed all the donations to a special fund called Maria's Miracle Fund. They found that over the following year $800,000 poured in and they decided to dedicate that fund to support the new 128-bed home in Luoyang, China.

In memory of Maria, they decided to name the home Maria's Big House of Hope.

It was very hard for the family to pick themselves up and get on with daily life while they were still grieving. They kept going, supported by the love and prayers of family and friends, but it was a very hard year, trying to come to terms with the loss of Maria.

22

Every child counts

God said, "I am their DADDY, and every child is important to Me."

Amy Eldridge

Some months earlier, an old Chinese friend of the Hills called Marsha at New Hope with a plea for help. She had been to visit another CWI in Henan province and was left distraught by the needs of the sick and terminally ill children there.

"Please can you get your bosses to go down to Xinyang and try and help?" she asked Marsha.

Rob and Joyce visited the CWI and decided, with the director's blessing and with the approval and support of the Board of Directors and friends of New Hope, to open a third palliative care unit there immediately. So, just after the first foundations were dug for the new 128-bed home in Luoyang, work also began on a unit in Xinyang. Simon Wu once again offered to manage the renovations, and twelve weeks later they were able to open the new Xinyang unit. The eighteen beds were immediately filled with the terminally ill babies that Joyce had not been allowed to see up to that point.

The Hills were now responsible for not only the main foster home in Beijing, but also three special care and palliative units in

Henan, which included the unit in the CWI in Jiaozuo, the unit in the Luoyang CWI – which they were busy replacing with the new 128-bed home – and now a further special care unit in the CWI in Xinyang.

At the same time as opening the third unit, the Hills also helped to set up a palliative care unit in a CWI on Hainan Island, some 2,500 miles away in the South.

Because of the distances involved, they explained to the director there that New Hope Foundation would not be able to run and manage that unit. The CWI would manage it themselves with funds promised by a couple in the USA who were friends of Marsha. New Hope Foundation was able, however, to offer to provide heart surgery for two of their children, who have since been healed and adopted.

In the meantime, there was also great news for Toby Isaiah, who had been treated by Joyce for club foot. He had been approved for adoption and his new family was making plans to come out and collect him. His new mum and dad were both pastors and had a large family of both biological and adopted children waiting to welcome him. He would be going to live out in the countryside in the USA, in a log cabin with an orchard of apple trees. But while Toby Isaiah was waiting for his new parents to arrive, he was recalled to his old CWI for official reasons, along with his new best buddy, Howie. They were to be away from their foster home so suddenly, and Joyce felt for them greatly. She knew that Toby's new family would soon be able to pick him up, but it was going to be hard for Howie once Toby was gone. Howie was a sweet little boy with Down's syndrome, and he and Toby had been cared for by the same two nannies and now had cots right next to each other in the CWI and felt glad to have each other's company. It just seemed a pity that Howie was unlikely to ever get adopted.

Howie had had a rough start in life. He was abandoned in a forest and a worker found him in the snow, wrapped in just a sheet. The worker and his wife cared for him for a day and had then taken him to the police station. When Howie was taken to the CWI a local care worker brought him to Joyce to fix the baby's clubbed foot, since she knew that Joyce was able to carry out the procedure at New Hope. Joyce had already been told that Howie had Down's syndrome, but when she examined the baby she realized that he also had an undiagnosed bowel condition and was dangerously ill. The care worker was shocked that no one had noticed such a major problem, but she was able to help Joyce arrange for a hospital to take Howie straight in for emergency surgery.

Once he came out of hospital, Howie came to live at New Hope Foster Home. Joyce was not expecting him ever to be adopted, since few people asked for a little boy like Howie, but that was not the end of the story.

While Mary Beth was staying at New Hope, she and Howie had a thumbs-up game going, and Howie was pictured in an article about China and New Hope in one of Show Hope's newsletters in the USA. At that time, in the USA, a couple called Liz and Dan Kulp had applied to adopt a child from China, but Dan was feeling nervous about becoming a first-time dad. After attending a Steven Curtis Chapman concert, Dan received the Show Hope newsletter about adoption, and in it was a picture of Howie, a Down's syndrome child, sweet and handsome and totally himself.

Dan had grown up with a younger brother who had Down's syndrome and his mum had gone on to adopt three further Down's children. He was used to helping take care of his siblings, and was comfortable with their needs. Dan says, "I didn't think

I knew how to be a dad, but when I saw Howie, I thought, 'Yes, I do know how to be a dad!'" He excitedly went and showed Liz the article and told her that seeing Howie had made him realize he felt confident and comfortable about adopting and caring for a child.

Some time later Liz and Dan decided that they wanted to apply to specifically adopt a child with Down's syndrome. The child that Liz and Dan were matched with was Howie. It seemed to Joyce to be a match made in heaven, both for Howie and for this wonderful couple.

Two years later, Liz and Dan returned to China to adopt a second child, this time a daughter. Liz says, "We spent the day with the couple who cared for Howie on that first day – quite an amazing day for our family!"

Howie's parents also made contact with Toby Isaiah's family and now regularly meet up with the Linn family so that the boys can still keep in touch.

As the Hills began to save more and more babies once classified as dying, they realized that some of the children would have continuing special needs, and that not many of those children would get adopted. So they decided that two of the floors in Maria's Big House should be dedicated to caring for those children. The hope was to keep them there until they were five years old, by which time they would be stronger and have a better chance of thriving in the more challenging situation of a CWI.

Joyce and Robin felt that they should continue to keep their focus on saving lives, and on caring for those babies who were dying. But with the Chapmans, they prayed and hoped that new people would come on board with a vision to work with and care for children who would rarely be put forward for adoption by official channels.

One couple already working in Beijing with the long-term needs of orphans are Delphine and Guillaume Gauvain. After living in China for six years they rented a seventeen-acre farm just outside Beijing, where they now have seven family-sized homes, sympathetically built to resemble a small village of log cabins. Here, they are able care for up to seventy blind orphans aged between two and twenty-two. In the main building nearby – once the private residence of an official – they have opened a school, a clinic and a training centre where the children can learn the skills they need to become as independent as possible.

"So far as we know," says Guillaume, "there is no one else doing this sort of work here in China."

Delphine and Guillaume felt that they should set up a home specifically for abandoned babies and children who were also blind and so were totally unable to protect themselves. They visited Robin and Joyce to pick up as many tips as they could on setting up a home for children. Guillaume was canny enough to see that there was no point in reinventing the wheel; it was better to emulate what was working and so conserve energy for innovations.

Visiting the Bethel home for blind children today, it feels something like a relative of New Hope, with the same bright rooms and well-organized systems, storerooms and medical rooms, and the same colour-coding so that the nannies can keep each child's possessions personal. Above all, it has the same spirit of expecting the very highest standard of care for every child.

Guillaume and Delphine have put in place innovative sensory and training programmes to help the children realize their potential. Some of the children have come from abusive situations, some being used for begging and then abandoned, and so Delphine has also brought in counsellors for those who need to regain confidence in life.

As the children grow into more independence they are able to move into the family units in the log cabins and consider training for possible careers.

Guillaume and Delphine have limitless energy in their quest to do all they can for the children. The home is self-sufficient in fresh vegetables and they are planning to produce their own goat's cheese. The main building hums with songs, arts and crafts projects, and teaching sessions where the children learn skills from reading Braille to learning to fold and care for their own clothes. Bethel has recently added stables and a horse to allow for hippotherapy (horse riding as therapy) – especially effective for the blind children that they care for who are also autistic. Guillaume enjoys telling any visiting children to watch out for the hippo as they get a tour of the farm!

Delphine and Guillaume have three children – Emily, Benjamin and David, who was born with a cleft palate. David's birth parents were Chinese. Delphine says that she feels incredibly blessed that David is now her son and can meet his new family in France.

Delphine and Guillaume are pioneering a new respect for blind children and are now working towards taking the Bethel programme into all CWIs. They have begun holding training sessions to enable CWI staff to give blind children the care they need and deserve to lead fulfilled lives.

* * *

Joyce and Robin say that since they have been caring for children with a range of special needs, whether treatable or long-term, they have come to understand that it is all too easy to be blind to the fact that every child has the right to be loved, respected and cared for.

Sometimes, simply being willing to see children with special needs as people rather than problems is enough to have far-reaching effects. While she was at a Show Hope event in Nashville in November 2008, Joyce was amazed to be handed a note by a stranger, about a little boy she had never met. Having given Joyce the note, which was written on the back of a programme, the woman walked away without a word. The note read:

Dear Robin and Joyce,

I couldn't help but write this now on the paper that I have at hand. Just last March, my husband and I travelled with a few friends to see Hope Healing Home. That visit completely changed my heart towards adopting a child with special needs. I had said, "No way can we do that – we just don't have the resources." But your home and your faith made me see.

I heard, "You don't have to be afraid."

And so we adopted T, unafraid of his bladder exstrophy… and failed surgeries, unafraid of his permanent urostomy and colostomy.

Oh, how we have been blessed by the love of this little boy who was rescued. T has rescued our hearts and we have both of you to thank for the most part.

Your example of faith made it OK for us to venture, afraid but unfearful into the unknown. Thank you and thank you.

SAC

23

Holding on

God abundantly provides for the things He wants to do.
ROBIN HILL

As the Luoyang building was nearing completion, the news in the papers and on TV was suddenly all about the banking crisis in Europe and America, soon becoming a global issue.

Over the next few months, instead of having the usual three or four months' running costs in the bank, Robin and Joyce saw that they only had enough for one month. It was not a comfortable margin.

And yet they were able to keep on paying all the salaries each month, go ahead with the surgeries needed, and continue with their plans to move the babies out of the Luoyang fifth-floor unit and into Maria's Big House of Hope. Rob commented to Joyce, "We might not have quite such a big security blanket as before it started, but it doesn't seem to affect our economy in God's eyes."

Of course, they did find themselves worrying from time to time: with so many children, they now had very large overheads, and the question "What if nothing happens for next month?" was always hovering in the background. But when a child came in needing urgent heart surgery, Joyce knew that she did not have time to stop and worry about making sure they had all the funds, so she just sent the child to get the help they needed. They found that many caring people continued throughout the economic situation to follow the children's progress and to step in when help was needed. Rob and Joyce's conclusion about a tough financial year is that "God can be trusted, even in what look like really bad circumstances."

"One of the things we have seen," Rob says, "is that God has provided abundantly for the things He wanted us to do here in China. We may see these abandoned kids as the 'least of the least', but God wants us to give them the best we can, and we see that over and over again."

The Hills found that they needed to trust through difficult times in other ways too. The past couple of years had been extremely busy for Joyce and Robin, and yet Joyce's health had often left her in pain and unable to do anything but lie prostrate on the sofa for the second half of each day.

Joyce had had eighteen months without any headaches after the first bout, but then they came back with a vengeance, and this time, they refused to go away. Joyce went for extensive tests in both Hong Kong and Singapore, and friends and family did all they could to suggest answers and prayed for Joyce, but she was not able to tell them that things were getting any better. The spinal leak continued so that when standing or sitting upright, she felt the pain of her brain pressing on the base of her skull.

Joyce had always got up early with the babies and completed her medical rounds and office work by lunchtime. She kept to this schedule, but by the end of each morning her headache was so intense that she was forced to lie down simply to relieve the pressure.

For someone as active as Joyce and with so much to do, this was not only painful, but also excruciatingly frustrating. She had seventy children to care for in New Hope Foster Home, and seventy-five children in the three palliative and special care units; decisions for the new home and operating theatre in Luoyang also needed to be carefully considered. She also had a large network of correspondence that she kept up with doctors all over the world to make surgical arrangements.

Joyce was desperate to find more medical personnel to help. She urgently needed to find a suitable doctor to help in Henan, at the units in Jiaozuo, Luoyang and Xinyang. But it was very difficult to find someone who understood both Western medicine and Chinese hospital procedures. She also needed someone fluent both in English and Chinese who was at a suitable stage in their family life where they could live in a local Chinese community for an extended period. Joyce knew that this last issue was very important, as in the past she had had long-term volunteers who were completely committed to stay and help in the homes in Henan, but whose children were unable to get used to the cultural demands of suddenly switching to a Chinese lifestyle. She needed someone who could also fit in with the frustrations and constraints of Chinese regulations, and who was prepared to be in a situation where Joyce stood as a line manager. Since there were so many issues to hold together, medically, financially, culturally and officially, it was essential for any staff to work as a team, under the umbrella of the approval that the Henan authorities had given to the Hills, if they were to continue to carry out the work with the children.

Marsha and Rob were always on hand to run the logistics of the homes and Joyce had several good nurses in all the units who were able to carry out the necessary medical procedures under her instruction, and until the new home opened in Luoyang all the serious cases for medical care were with Joyce in the home in

Beijing, but she urgently needed a doctor to be in place in Henan before the new 128-bed home opened. She could not understand why God was not sending the right person when she was struggling so much with her health and longing for some help.

One weekend Joyce also began to suffer pain in her knee. This seemed like the last straw. It was possibly a long-term arthritic problem, and Joyce felt very low and depressed. She said to God, "Why, when I am obeying you, and doing your work, and I have so much to do, why don't you heal me and let me get on with it?" They went to their church in a community hall near Beijing, but Joyce was very unhappy. She had so much to do; she was responsible for so many children. Why was God letting this happen?

But as she sat in the service she began to feel more peaceful. She felt that God was giving her an answer. All she was being asked to do was obey Him, and He would do the rest. So she went home, still in pain, but more at peace that God would provide the help she needed.

Her knee improved, but the headaches continued. Robin rigged up a computer screen so that Joyce could lie down flat on the sofa and do her work. As an engineer Rob always enjoyed building things and felt rather proud of his handiwork. He called Joyce in to have a look at what he had done for her. She stood and admired it, but when they caught each other's eye they both burst out crying. They knew that it symbolized that Joyce's headache was now chronic. It was going to be a long-term condition and it wasn't going to go away.

And yet, Rob says in retrospect, the fact that Joyce had been affected by her illness helped in some ways. It made them re-evaluate Joyce's role and pull her back to a more overseeing position so that they were ready to expand. So in the year before

Maria's Big House opened, Joyce was working hard to see how she might delegate various jobs to other staff. But for that to actually happen, she needed to have the medical staff. And soon.

After a year of searching, Joyce found Dr Zhai. He was born not far from Luoyang and had worked in the USA as a research fellow into rare childhood illnesses at the Vanderbilt Children's hospital in Nashville – the same hospital where the Hills had taken Katie and Molly for surgery. Rob got to hear about Dr Zhai and asked for his advice on buying equipment for the new home. When Rob outlined to him some of the work they were doing in Henan, Dr Zhai was extremely enthusiastic and interested, and the Hills decided to ask if he would like to consider coming on board. Dr Zhai began helping with the three palliative care units and agreed to help care for the children in Maria's Big House when it opened.

Joyce was also relieved to find that she was able to hire some excellent nurses from the Philippines to fill the new roles in Maria's Big House.

Joyce says, "I was getting more and more tired, and unable to cope physically. I kept thinking, 'Lord, just bring some more people. I can't do this any more.' And all of a sudden I have all these people here – a second doctor, and new nurses. I have been able to delegate and we can carry on working." With the help of the Chapman family, the many supporters of New Hope, and the new members of staff, they now had a team to help carry the work forward – in spite of Joyce's poor health and a tricky financial climate due to a world financial recession.

Over the course of the past year, it had sometimes felt as if they were being bumped around in choppy waters, but as they looked back, it was clear to Joyce and Robin that they had been carried along to a new place and given amazing and unprecedented opportunities to help needy children, especially within China's Henan province. Robin and Joyce were acutely aware that the needs they had seen were replicated across all Henan with its huge population of over 100 million people. If Henan were a country rather than a province, then it would be the thirteenth most populous in the world, coming just after Mexico. It seemed a dream of impossible proportions, but Joyce and Robin were now asking themselves if there was some way to reach every sick or dying child abandoned in that province.

24

Maria's Big House of Hope

If you can't hold children in your arms, please hold them in your heart.

CLARA HALE

By August 2008 Maria's Big House was nearing completion. Rob was having very frustrating talks with the team of builders who were installing the septic tank. They insisted that it could be placed uphill from the home because, once it was full, the waste would flow upwards into the tank. Rob was rendered speechless. In the end, the situation could only be resolved by Rob sacking the workmen and bringing in a new team.

However, Rob and Xiao Ying, the foreman from Simon Wu's firm, were still able to go round and discuss colour schemes while the huge concrete shell of the building rang with metal clangs and the whirr of drills. Across the muddy area that would one day be the playground, another building was also going up. This was the replacement CWI to rehouse the 700 children in the state CWI. The Hills' new home would continue to be closely connected with the main CWI, and they would be on hand to reach any children that needed help.

Scott Hasenbalg came over several times to see how the project was progressing. He and the Hills were now firm friends, as was the case with another regular visitor from Steven's crew, David Trask. Rob and David had the same wicked but dry sense of humour and the same skill of gently but firmly making sure that what should get done, got done, while ending up as a friend and father figure to those around them. Dave says, "You know, I've worked for people like Fleetwood Mac and had some pretty wild times, and I love road managing for Steven, but coming over here to work with Hope, that's the best time I've ever had." Rob and Dave drew up their own "bucket list" of things they wanted to do in their later years, and in November 2009, they both ticked off sky diving during a visit to Nashville.

In January 2009, the building was ready for a team from Show Hope, including Emily and her husband and her brother Caleb, to visit Luoyang and begin to put the baby beds together. Emily and the others also went to visit the children in the main CWI and made particular friends with a young boy named Will. He insisted on giving Emily a guided tour of the sleeping rooms, pointing out his own iron bunk bed. In the bare and scuffed room, there was nothing except these iron bunks. Will proudly showed Emily all his possessions: his pillows and a blanket.

Moving day arrived. A fleet of taxis with nannies carrying babies, and trucks of equipment, were kept busy under Linda's supervision, ferrying between the two homes. By the end of the day everyone was exhausted, but the nannies were evidently very proud to be in their new home and the children could sense their excitement.

But there was a problem. Official access to Maria's Big House was through a side road shared with the old people's home, yet the gatekeeper did not agree with this new arrangement for his road. He kept his gate firmly shut. When the nannies arrived for work the next morning, they had to negotiate a track on the other side, picking their way over flattened rubble.

Rob did all he could to settle the matter, but the gatekeeper still kept his gate resolutely shut. This was certainly going to be a big problem when 200 people arrived for the opening ceremony in a few weeks' time. So Rob took the decision to resurface the other road. The results had a rough-and-ready air, but at least they could now get in and out of the building.

* * *

In July 2009 all the Chapman family, along with close friends and supporters, arrived at Beijing Airport accompanied by huge quantities of luggage containing donations for Maria's Big House of Hope. They managed to retrieve all their bags in the airport with no problems, but as they were leaving they were stopped by airport officials. One of their party had registered a high temperature on the airport scanners, and according to the regulations for the Swine Flu epidemic, the entire party would all have to be quarantined at the home in Beijing for a week. They would not be able to fly to the opening of Maria's Big House in Luoyang on 2 July.

This was a bitter blow. The Chapmans were longing to be there together and celebrate the home that was due to be dedicated in Maria's name, but nothing could be done except wait.

They were very disappointed when clearance failed to arrive in time, and the Hills had to set off for the airport without Steven and Mary Beth. But on the way there Rob suddenly got a call from the local authorities giving the all clear for everyone to travel. The Hills rang home with the message: "Grab your stuff! We're all going!"

After some complicated travel rescheduling, about fifty people in total finally flew to Luoyang for the opening ceremony. Since the temperatures were soaring that week, Director Pei suggested that the ceremony begin as soon as possible before the temperatures became unbearable. So early next morning they all boarded several buses and drove out to Maria's Big House of Hope.

It was clearly visible from a distance, its bright blue walls and white clouds standing out in the hazy air across the wide river floodplain. As they drove past the garage opposite the home they saw that it had also been painted the same bright blue with sprayed-on clouds – possibly the beginning of a new fashion in Luoyang buildings, Rob remarked.

A brass band made up of some of the children from the main CWI, dressed smartly in khaki and red uniforms, was assembled to greet the guests. The CWI had arranged a long podium in front of the house, decorated with giant inflatable Chinese lanterns and a huge banner announcing the opening of Maria's Big House of Hope in Chinese lettering. Director Pei and his successor, and the directors from both the local and regional civil bureaux in Luoyang and Zhengzhou, gave several formal speeches in Mandarin. Mary Beth and Steven did not have enough Chinese to follow what was said, but picked out the word "Maria" – said often and with warm enthusiasm.

After the ceremony, all the guests went back to a Chinese banquet in the hotel with the Chinese officials. Robin and Joyce were very encouraged by all the support shown to them by the directors of the local civil affairs bureau during the opening ceremony. Rob felt that there had been a real feeling of trust from the Henan authorities; the Hills had come along with a proposal to open a new home, and now it was up and running well.

Later that afternoon, Robin went back with Steven, Mary Beth and their family and friends to Maria's Big House and they decided to do an impromptu prayer walk. Steven got his guitar and they walked through each room singing and praying together and with all the children joining in by dancing and clapping. They even covered the corridors and halls. At times the combined voices, amplified by the building, produced more than the sum of the few voices together. Rob says, "I will never forget the experience of standing and singing in the stairwells. It was like a sound tunnel of everyone singing praise and worship songs together."

Rob was only sad that Joyce had been unable to be there with them. In spite of high doses of her pain medication, she had needed to remain at the hotel and lie down after standing upright for so long.

A week after the official opening of Maria's Big House, a second group of volunteers arrived from the Show Hope Foundation in Nashville. They stayed with Rob and Joyce at New Hope for a few days and then took the overnight train from Beijing to give a hand at Maria's Big House.

There were twenty people in all booked into several berths along the train. Everything in China seems to take place on an epic scale, but the group managed to negotiate the vast halls of Beijing international train station where guards calmly shepherd thousands of people onto the right train from a series of enormous waiting rooms.

They settled four to a carriage, admiring the fresh white beds and the small table complete with a lace tablecloth. After a smooth twelve-hour run, the morning light showed fields and hills of yellow clay terraced into patches of maize, or copses of trees. Small communities of one-storey houses, with lines of washing drying in the morning mist, nestled together inside village walls, some with imposing traditional Chinese gateways, although many smallholders' homes had seemingly been abandoned as families had migrated to the towns.

Amber and her husband Marcio had come back to China for the summer to help Emily and her husband Tanner look after the volunteers – even travelling on a bus or ordering a meal can be taxing if you don't speak Chinese.

Mary Beth's brother Jim was one of the team and he came up with the idea of finishing off the sky-blue walls with a mural at ground-floor level. By the end of the first day the boys had painted the first coat of rolling green hills around the base of the building while in the hallway Jim had begun a scaled-up copy of the last painting done by Maria. She had not yet finished the picture on her painting desk, and only one of the petals had been coloured in bright blue. Jim knew that finding this picture had been a great comfort to Steven and Mary Beth. Beside the flower Maria had written the word "SEE" and it seemed to epitomize their hope and faith that they would see Maria again. Jim was hoping that this mural on the lobby wall would be the first thing that Mary Beth and Steven saw when they returned the next day. The Chapmans' hope and grief for Maria was now entwined with the hope of Maria's Big House: to save as many babies as possible, and to lovingly care for those who were passing away, their short lives unfinished to human eyes.

It was a source of sadness to the staff that in the week since they had moved into the new building, four of the very sick babies had passed away, too ill to be given any further intervention treatment. They had been made comfortable and loved and held by their nannies until they slipped away. Dr Zhai explained that although those losses in the first week had been hard, he had been very encouraged that a child sent to the unit in October as being "too ill to live" was now healthy and normal, following major surgery for a heart condition. A bright and pretty little girl called Michaela, she was already on the list to be adopted.

Several new children had arrived directly from the main CWI. Theo had come in very hungry, and had drunk the equivalent of seven feeds in one go. He was also very dirty and his rag-cloth nappy had been taped on and left. It was possible that Theo had not been given much help as he was not attractive to look at. He had a large head for his wasted body, his spine was curved, and his wisps of legs and feet were twisted outwards. But Theo had a wonderful engaging smile with a lovely sense of humour, and was now responding beautifully to his new nannies and friends.

After a long, hot day the guests and volunteers settled into their accommodation on the top floor for the night – a girls' and a boys' dorm. By the time they were up and dressed to start painting again, it was quite apparent which was which, one room being a sea of neat white duvets and folded clothes, and the other quite hard to describe.

When Mary Beth and Steven arrived later the next day, Jim Chapman was putting the final touches to Maria's painting in the hallway. It was evident that this gesture from her brother meant a great deal to Mary Beth. There were lots of hellos and catching up with everyone, and then Steven and Mary Beth visited the babies' rooms where some of the babies were already making their little personalities known. Yo-yo was keeping everyone busy with his mile-a-minute approach to life in spite of his restricted sight, and was charging around the playroom looking for new things to chew, which included someone's bag and someone else's knee.

The first floor of Maria's Big House would fulfil the same role as the Hope home in Beijing, with family rooms for those babies who had correctable medical needs. The children would need a lot of care and time to get better, as they could be extremely vulnerable after major surgery and often needed medical supervision to ensure that the visiting surgeons' hard work was followed through until the child was healthy. With the Luoyang first floor now open, Joyce would be able to double the number of children that they could help in this way.

The second and third floors were family rooms designed to take care of those children who had been saved and made a good recovery, but who had long-term conditions that meant that they were unlikely to be adopted.

The fourth floor was the palliative care unit for children who were terminally ill. All the children sent over from the CWI were diagnosed as terminal; they would be admitted into the palliative care floor and then assessed, and if the child was beyond medical help, then the baby would be given care and pain relief and would be allowed to die in peace and dignity. However, if there was any chance of saving them, then all options would be followed up as far as was reasonably possible. The hope was that in Maria's Big House they would continue to save many babies.

On the fifth floor there was a full surgical theatre for carrying out minor repairs, a dental room and enough beds to give intensive and post-operative nursing to sixteen children. Two delightful Filipina nurses called Erma and Jona were busy helping Dr Zhai set up the equipment and beds, along with medical students volunteering from the USA and from Cambridge in the UK. There was also a large room that could host conferences and training sessions where staff from other CWIs would be able to attend courses.

The top floor held pleasant accommodation for the permanent medical staff, and also for visiting doctors and volunteers.

One of the great joys for everybody was the news that four of the babies had already been approved for adoption, including little mile-a-minute Yo-yo. The nurses Jona and Erma had to spend some time getting him to stand still long enough for them to take his passport picture ready to travel out with his new mum and dad.

As the hot summer's day came to a close, the volunteers assembled in the downstairs hall, ready to take a bus into town to have supper in the new shopping centre in the middle of Luoyang. One party was opting for a traditional Chinese meal following Dr Zhai's expertise in ordering from a Chinese menu, and others were going to hunt out the delights of McDonald's.

As Amber and Emily herded their group of tired volunteers out of the doors, they passed the night nannies coming in to look after the babies through till morning. One last look back at the hallway showed a frieze of Maria's daisies stencilled around the walls, each one standing out palely in the evening light. The vibrant but unfinished flowers seemed to wordlessly express something of the pain that the Father feels, each time a precious child passes away; and how in Him there is hope for the painting to be finished.

Steven says of Maria's Big House of Hope: "Children are comforted as they are dying. Children are growing healthy. Out of the pain and loss of losing Maria there's that hopeful, beautiful thing that's blooming in that place."

25

A special birthday

May the God of hope fill you with all joy and peace as you trust in him, so that you may overflow with hope by the power of the Holy Spirit.

ROMANS 15:13

On a hot day in August 2009, the Hills were enjoying a quiet lull before welcoming the next group of visitors. The yurts stood empty again at the edge of the maize field, like three large and dusty birthday cakes, and while the nannies were giving the babies lunch in the dining room, Katie came in carrying a real birthday cake: a huge pink-and-blue confection decorated with sugar roses to share with all the nannies and babies. It was Katie's tenth birthday.

Ten years earlier, the Hills had assembled a baby's cot in their dining room with Amber and Ryan eagerly helping. Shortly after that, Katie came home. Now Katie was their own adopted daughter, and the Hills had cared for a total of over 600 children, with 93 of the babies going forward to be adopted by their own forever families.

Joyce and Robin, Amber and Marcio took Katie out for a birthday lunch at her favourite pizza restaurant. They returned in the afternoon to a hushed home, the babies all napping on their sleeping mats, little arms thrown out in the cool air conditioning while the nannies took a welcome breather and chatted quietly.

Katie and her friend ran off for a dip in the plunge pool, leaving one of Rob's music tapes playing in the kitchen. A fish splashed lazily in the pool in the entrance hall and outside in the garden the cicadas kept up their sleepy chorus. Always visible through the windows of the house were the memorial wall, and the willow tree planted over Nico's ashes.

The Hills say that of all the babies they have cared for, it was Nico who really helped them understand God's attitude to those children who are counted as the "least of the least". Nico was one of the most severely handicapped babies that Joyce and Robin had ever known. He was unable to see, hear, move or respond. He truly was the least of the least – in human eyes. But, says Rob, God viewed Nico differently. Joyce offered to look after Nico at New Hope, not really knowing how she would provide for his complex, special needs, yet everything she needed to give the baby the best medical help and to provide nannies who would be with him day and night was immediately supplied by people who chose to care about him.

Rob says, "It was one of the things that really hit me; how God was willing to put all of the very best resources around a child that was never going to amount to anything in this lifetime. It always spoke to me; if God was willing to do that for Nico, then how much more is God willing to do that for all of us – to just wastefully expend His grace for each of us, throughout eternity?"

Joyce also feels that it was Nico who drew around him some of their most vital helpers and supporters in those early days, people who became instrumental in supporting the later growth of the home and in caring for many more children.

By the time Christmas 2009 came round, Beijing was

experiencing its coldest winter for fifteen years, with temperatures sometimes down to minus 20 degrees. But inside New Hope and Maria's Big House the children were warm, and only too delighted to get the chance to go out and play in the snow.

At New Year, Rob and Joyce were able to take Katie to visit Amber and Marcio in London and they also visited the grave of Rob's dad. The children honoured their family custom of leaving a nice cup of tea ready on granddad's headstone.

In 2010, the Hills were given two further opportunities to reach more babies in Henan province. The director of the original SCU that they had opened in Jiaozuo was rebuilding the entire CWI and now wanted Joyce to use one of the floors in the new institution so that she could increase the number of palliative care beds from twelve to thirty-six.

The second opportunity was something that they had only dared to dream of for a long time, and could influence childcare policy throughout the whole of the province. The director of the central CWI in Henan's capital city, Zhengzhou, wanted them to open a new special care unit for babies in his CWI who were considered to be terminally ill, and care for fifty of the sickest children. The new Zhengzhou special care unit was a really significant development, and soon the Hills found that they were being asked by many more CWIs in Henan to come and start similar units.

Joyce and Robin flew from Beijing to visit the Zhengzhou CWI and discuss plans with the director. Simon Wu and the Littlewoods also flew out as part of the installation team. The CWI was a pleasant low-rise building, just two years old, with a large garden at its centre. It was surrounded by peach orchards and had the botanical gardens nearby. The children looked well cared for and clean. But the home had a problem: they received around 100 infants each year with serious medical issues. There was a high mortality rate. The director was happy for the Hills to begin work immediately. With such enthusiasm from the director, they would be able to have the new unit up and running in a few months.

Before flying back to Beijing, Robin, Joyce and the Littlewoods took the chance to visit the ancient Song Dynasty capital of Kaifeng. They were treated to a spectacular solar eclipse above the flood plains of the Yellow River. It was reckoned to be the longest eclipse for the next 1,000 years.

It was also a chance to reflect on how much that had seemed impossible ten years ago had gradually happened. It still seemed a lot to ask, but it was also the prayer of the Hills that the model in Henan might one day be replicated across the whole country. Director Pei had already twice hosted days in which CWI directors came from provinces all over China to see the work in Luoyang. "What we really pray for," says Joyce, "is that one day we will no longer be needed."

* * *

Robin and Joyce were now in their early sixties. They had a total of 300 employees, and with the new units they would be caring for over 338 children at any one time. By February of 2010 Joyce was staggered to note that they had cared for some 795 babies and children. The numbers were daunting, but they also had no doubt that God would give them the energy, the help and the funds they needed to see the next step through.

Over the years Joyce and Robin had seen people from all over the world take the children into their hearts in both small ways and in big ways. Whether it was one schoolchild raising money to send a gift to a baby, a family sponsoring a particular child, doctors giving their time and skills to save lives, or a large company making a substantial donation, they had seen so many people come together to make what Joyce called "God's jigsaw", where every piece was essential to save the life of one more child.

Robin and Joyce were also keenly aware that they had been greatly blessed by meeting such friends as Steven and Mary Beth Chapman, Amy Eldridge and Dr Ngan – people with the same heart to save lives and to make a difference to the future of needy and abandoned babies. As the summer ended, thousands of miles away in Nashville, Scott Hasenbalg, the executive director from Show Hope, was busy holding meetings with doctors from Geisinger Medical Center in Danville, Pennsylvania, to organize the first medical mission trips to carry out surgeries at Maria's Big House of Hope. The Chapmans and Show Hope were also hard at work linking sponsors with the new babies arriving in Maria's Big House. Through partnerships with MedArt, China Orphans Outreach, Love Without Boundaries, and Show Hope, the Hills had been able to help an ever-increasing number of sick and disabled children.

It was apparent to Joyce and Robin that they had moved from being a small "mom and pop" organization, where they managed every detail of each unit, to being overseers of something too large for one or two pairs of hands. They took the decision that it would be helpful to invite the Board of the New Hope Foster Home, all of whom were very dear friends and who had supported the home in every way possible, to have equal votes in decision making.

With so many hands on board they were able to contemplate new large-scale projects. The new SCU unit in Henan's capital was due to open on schedule, so Joyce sent out a message via the online newsletter to let people know that the particular need for that month was going to be for baby clothes – over the next few weeks, a hundred new babies would be arriving.

As the years had gone by, Robin and Joyce had found it a great blessing to see their combined family of seven surviving children moving into various careers and enjoying their own new families, and they were both immensely grateful for the way the children had all supported their decision to stay on in China.

Joyce and Robin were surprised to get the news that Joyce's eldest son Adam, a lawyer, had entered the Australian Master Chef competition. Ruth, Adrian and Ryan were also living and working in Australia and so were able to follow his progress week by week on TV, culminating in Adam winning the title – along with quite a following nationwide. He had evidently put time into watching his Chinese granny cook over the years and his food was an artful blend of Chinese and European ingredients.

Life had also come full circle in an interesting way for Amber. She was now studying medicine in Kuala Lumpur, the same city where Joyce had once been a medical student some forty years earlier. Aron was continuing with medical training, and Katie was enjoying senior school in Beijing, although very frustrated to see Joyce so ill each day.

Out of the blue, Joyce received a phone call from the Australian Embassy informing her that she was going to be presented with a decoration in the Queen's Birthday Honours. She had no idea how this had come about but it was a great encouragement. Here was another reminder of the tremendous goodwill and support that came to the Hills and the babies of New Hope Foster Home from all across the world. Katie showed how well she had taken on her parents' values by suggesting they should sell the medal and so help more children. Joyce was amazed to also hear that the embassy was going to earmark 80,000 Australian dollars from their development fund to help the New Hope babies. In

February, Joyce went to the Australian Embassy in Beijing to collect the award. Although, she told Rob, the only award that Joyce truly cared for was to know that she had done all she could for the children in her care, and to hear the words one day, "Well done, good and faithful servant."

Joyce visited Hong Kong twice over the following few months to see if the headaches could be alleviated by patching her spinal leaks with blood clots. It had been a difficult decision to go through the painful intervention procedures once more and continue to hope for some relief. She said, "Prayers had been said again and again by so many, all over the world, and yet no healing was in sight. And so I had accepted that, for whatever reason, God was not healing me. It would be in His time and by His grace that healing would occur, and if He chose not to heal me, I was fine with that as well." But for the sake of Katie and Rob, who had prayed long and hard to see her get better, Joyce decided to try and see if something could be done.

Using advanced equipment and his increased knowledge of such a rare condition, the specialist in Hong Kong was able to locate six leaks along her spine. The next day the operation was performed. Joyce was amazed to find that her headaches were relieved within minutes. Flying back from Hong Kong a few days later, she braced herself for the usual excruciating pain as the aircraft landed. But there was absolutely no pain. Joyce did not know whether to laugh or cry.

The pain was absent for a few weeks, but then returned. Joyce had a further trip to Hong Kong to attempt to patch the leaks, but the operation was not successful. Joyce and Rob were very disappointed to have to face that the headaches were going to remain an ongoing problem. "We can only hope," said Rob, "that there will be a cure at some point in the future."

Joyce was glad that in spite of the pain she was still able to continue to care for the children, managing an increasing team of helpers and getting most tasks done before the pain took over and she had to lie down for the latter part of the day.

Joyce says, "I have no real words of wisdom about my experience. I just know that if He has chosen someone specially to be His servant, He will put you through hard times (expect it and embrace it). But He will always be by your side. I know that this experience has allowed my husband to demonstrate his love for me to an extent that I had never imagined possible."

On 22 October, Chaya, an abandoned baby with huge, trusting eyes, was admitted to New Hope. The baby had a small lump under her chin and multiple birth defects, but Joyce was committed to do everything possible to bring the little girl into full health, and considered it a gift to be able to care for her.

Chaya was their one thousandth child and represented a little milestone in the Hills' work – although it was hardly a cause for celebration in their eyes. They would have much preferred to see fewer children in need. It was certainly hard to believe that the cot they had got ready for just one little girl all those years ago, had turned into 1,000 children being welcomed into their family at New Hope.

As 2011 approaches, ten years have gone by since Joyce and Robin felt they were being asked to step into a river and begin a new life – without knowing exactly where it was going to take them. Since then, they have been swirled around a few times, and even had to shoot some white-knuckle rapids, physically, emotionally and spiritually, but they have entrusted their lives to that river of love that flows from God's heart, and in doing so have seen God's love and provision for the least of the least, the orphans of China. Time after time, they have seen the evidence of how much God wants to provide abundantly and even extravagantly for the discarded and the abandoned. Rob says, "In His eyes, these children are the world's treasure and right up there, with the greatest in the land."

Rob and Joyce remain adamant, however, that they are far from super-spiritual people: they are just an ordinary couple who decided to say "yes" to what God wanted to do. They are also adamant that the invitation to jump in that river, and see where it takes you, is open to every ordinary person, and that if you choose to make that leap, it may be a shock to the system, but God can be trusted to do what He wants to do. Rob says, "It is possible to spend your whole life focusing on your own comfort and safety, or you can accept God's invitation to come into that river of His amazing love."

Sponsors and friends of New Hope Foundation

We wish to thank all those sponsors and friends who have helped us in the past and those who will continue to do so in the future:

Aldridge Parish Church
http://aldridgeparishchurch.org

AusAID
http://www.ausaid.gov.au

Beijing BISS International School
http://www.biss.com.cn

Beijing International Christian Fellowship
http://www.bicf.org

Beijing Quilters

Bethel Foster Home
http://www.bethelchina.org

Bosch
http://www.bosch.com.cn

The British Club
http://www.britishclub.org.sg

British Embassy Beijing
http://ukinchina.fco.gov.uk/en

Capital Community Congregation
http://www.capitalcommunitychurch.org

CEO Foundation
http://ceofoundation.site90.com

Child-Link
http://www.child-link.org.uk

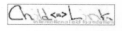

ChinaKidz
http://www.chinakidz.org

China Little Flower
http://www.chinalittleflower.org

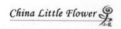

Chinese Children Adoption International
http://www.chinesechildren.org

Chinese Orphans' Assistance Team
http://www.eagleswingschina.org

COCOA (Care Of China's Orphaned and Abandoned children)
http://www.cocoa.org.uk

Dulwich College Beijing
http://www.dcbeijing.cn

Emmaus Road Ministries
http://www.emmausroad.org.nz

Excellence in Giving
http://www.excellenceingiving.com

GE
http://www.ge.com

German Christmas Bazaar

Giveline
http://www.giveline.com

Gladney Center for Adoption
http://www.adoptionsbygladney.com

Global Development Group
http://globaldevelopment.org.au

Harrow International School Beijing
http://www.harrowbeijing.cn

Hope's Heart Orphan Foundation
http://www.hopesheart.org

International School of Beijing
http://www.isb.bj.edu.cn

International SOS
http://www.internationalsos.com/en

Jones Day
http://www.jonesday.com

KK Women's and Children's Hospital
http://www.kkh.com.sg

Lafarge
http://www.lafarge.com

Leaders' Quest
http://www.leadersquest.org

Love Without Boundaries
http://www.lovewithoutboundaries.com

Matilda International Hospital
http://www.matilda.org

MedArt
http://www.medart.org.hk

A Mother's Love
http://www.amotherslovechina.com

NU2YU Baby Shop
http://www.nu2yubabyshop.com

Open Arms to International Adoption
http://www.open-arms.com

Portion for Orphans
http://www.portionfororphans.org

Primavera
http://www.primavera-ev.de

Procter & Gamble China
http://www.pg.com.cn

Revival Fires
http://revivalfires.org.uk

ROCA Chauffage
http://www.rt2000-chauffage.com

Sandvik
http://www.sandvik.com

Shell China
http://www.shell.com.cn

Show Hope
http://www.showhope.org

SKF
http://www.skf.com

TTc
http://www.talent-trust.com

United Family Healthcare
www.unitedfamilyhospitals.com/en/bj

UPS
http://www.ups.com

Virgin
www.virgin.com

Western Academy of Beijing
http://www.wab.edu

Xian-Janssen Pharmaceutical Ltd.
http://www.xian-janssen.com.cn

How can you get involved with New Hope Foundation's work in China?

Please go to their website: www.hopefosterhome.com

You will find information about volunteering, visiting and supporting them in many different ways.

If you would like to support them financially, please visit this website: **www.hopefosterhome.com/donations.htm**

The above website will give you all the information you will need to get tax benefits in Australia, Canada, Hong Kong, the UK and the USA. It also has information about donations via credit card.